Towards Dance and Art

Towards Dance and Art

A STUDY OF RELATIONSHIPS BETWEEN TWO ART FORMS

Elizabeth Watts

Lecturer in the Art of Movement
Keswick Hall College of Education
Norwich

LEPUS BOOKS
LONDON

© 1977 Lepus Books
An associate company of Henry Kimpton Ltd
7 Leighton Place, Leighton Road,
London NW5 2QL

ISBN 0 86019 027 7

Phototypesetting by Print Origination,
Bootle, Merseyside L20 6NS

Printed by Cambridge University Press

Contents

v

activity – primordial circle – not 'roundness' but
'thingness' (Arnheim) – visual perception and
imagery, for solidity, distinction, and shape.

associated perceptions – physiological activity –
visual, aural, tactile stimuli provide motivation for
imitation – 'gesture' extended to include facial,
vocal, whole-body gesture – emphasis on
kinaesthetic awareness – functional activities – the
body itself a means of expression – function of
drawing activities – a function of kinaesthetic
awareness – sensitivity to bodily state – 'good
feelings' prolonged – movement memory – 'total
bodily stir' (Laban) – impulse and spontaneity –
controlled, descriptive movements – educating for
understanding movement expression – feelings –
common physical element – emotion – emotion
observed – movements which reveal –
communication – common visual medium – but
visual factor irrelevant to rhythm and flow in
spontaneous dance – unlike art.

moving and looking differentiated – ends more than
means – the manner of looking – pleasure in moving
– becoming a listener – the expressively-intent
dancer – shapes, patterns, qualities of movement –
contrasting movement characteristics and tensions –
aesthetic and emotional response – communication
– the actor-dancer – 'linear' artists and descriptive
movements – the artist's perception.

moving and looking a continuous partnership –
moving 'in the service of' looking – three aspects of
dance – expressively-intent dance autonomous,
uniquely personal – the theatre, not the arena –
dance technique – 'artistic play' and work – stimuli
from other media – integration or parasitism – action
painting – rhythmically-stressed dance – its
developing function – present-day social dance –
parallels between rhythmically-stressed dance and

Acknowledgements

The author would like to acknowledge the permission given by those publishers and authors named in the list of references at the end of this book, for the use of copyright material which supports the text: in particular for the permission given by Dr Desmond Morris, whose study of ape paintings has been extensively quoted, and some of whose book plates have been reproduced here in black and white; and for the guidance and encouragement given by Mrs Lee Krasner Pollock. Thanks are due also to Dr Morris's publishers, Methuen; to Dr Robertson and to Thames and Hudson, and to the owners of paintings acknowledged in the legends.

Central to the book's development has been the work done in both movement and painting by many groups of children throughout the past twelve years. Special mention is due to a group of children at Woodside Middle School, Norwich, where the headmaster, Mr Sellick, and members of his staff have accepted a regular Friday invasion of student teachers and their tutor for several months, and given much help and encouragement; and to two groups of children at Northfields First School in Norwich, whose headmistress, Miss Alden, and staff have been most cooperative. The results of this cooperation are evident, in part, in the growing collection of children's paintings, a few of which form illustrative material in this book.

Thanks are due to a number of people who have helped to clarify and focus the author's thinking in recent years: to the former Director of the Art of Movement Studio, Miss Lisa Ullmann, and her staff – in particular Mr Roderyk Lange whose task it was to guide the original thesis for this book; and to colleagues at Keswick Hall who are prepared to engage in an on-going dialogue about the nature of the arts and the concept of a fundamental relationship between them.

Finally, the author wishes to acknowledge the time and thought given by two people who read the text: Mr Eric Hopkins, Principal Lecturer in Psychology at Keswick Hall; and Dr Geoffrey Watts, the author's husband.

Introduction ·

We hear much these days about integrated arts courses, combined arts courses, related arts courses – the implication being that, by association, music, dance, drama, and the visual arts may somehow vindicate the saying that the whole is greater than the sum of its parts. On a practical level, the simple physical proximity of working areas for each of the arts may stimulate joint projects; on a social level, the musician, the dancer, the artist and the actor may better understand each other's aims and needs, as may the composer, the choreographer and the dramatist; on a personal level, the individual may encounter ideas and experiences which enrich his life. But such benefits could be claimed for associating music with mathematics, and visual art with environmental sciences; and it is doubtful whether the whole would, in either case, be greater than the sum of its parts.

Perhaps a combined arts course claims no more than this as its right to exist. But an integrated arts course suggests a concept of a whole which would be incomplete without one of its parts, and of parts which would be merely raw material away from the whole – like cloth woven in several colours on both warp and weft, so that if you then remove one colour entirely you destroy both the pattern and the soundness of the cloth. Such a concept is exciting, challenging, and all-embracing; it cuts through the traditional isolation of departments built upon disciplines; it demands new attitudes towards the purpose of education and training in schools and colleges; and it exposes its participators to constant self-questioning.

The gallant enthusiasts whose instincts lead them to believe

1

in the viability, indeed the inevitability, of the integrated arts course are those who would have us all 'jump in at the deep end' – for many people, the only successful introduction to a formerly alien element! So the course is set up; (to revert to the analogy of the swimming pool) non-swimmers will find brisk and confident gold-medallists in the twelve-foot end who exhort them to swim, or tread water, or let themselves float – secure in the conviction that immersion in experience is the best, if not the only way, to discover what integrating the arts is all about. Perhaps they are right; but for many of us there is a need for a step-by-step introduction to fundamental relationships between the arts – if indeed such things exist. Are we, perhaps, in our enthusiasm, integrating the outer phenomena of the arts – sculptural shapes and trailing ribbons with sophisticated lighting effects to stimulate dance; music composed after contemplation of a picture; dramatic interplay inspired by masks; and costume and décor to enhance theatrical production? Are we integrating forms of expression which art educators like Sir Herbert Read carefully differentiated, and for which he postulated educational techniques in design, music and dance, poetry and drama, and craft – these four functions corresponding with the four mental processes of sensation, intuition, feeling, and thought?

Or are we attempting to begin with the individual, from his first apprehension of the world around him as a baby, and, through his exploration of himself and his environment, discover how far integration may encourage development at many levels, and whether there comes a time of over-riding need for the pursuit of separate disciplines?

Some years ago, I attended an Educational Conference-Course on 'Dance and the Arts'. We were divided into three groups according to our particular inclinations, to study Dance and Drama, Dance and Music, or Dance and Art. Relationships were implied, though not assumed; and the common interest lay in the consideration of the place of Dance in Education. Dance, music, and drama are dynamic events, happening in time – over as soon as they have begun, though capable of replay. The visual arts are, in the main, static phenomena, capable of unhurried contemplation. It was possible to conceive of a working relationship between dance and music, and between dance and drama; less easy between dance and art. Since I was, at that time, teaching both dance and art in a secondary school (but outside the requirements of examination courses) I found many links between the two subjects; in choice of language to stimulate desired responses; in presenting new ways of looking at familiar objects; in motivating mastery of technique; and generally to supply a vast source of imagery. I felt that such links might have a common origin, capable of being objectified in order that the source might be tapped consciously and to order. Hopefully, I chose the Dance/Art group.

During the course of our introductory talk, the coordinating art tutor took up his position and remained impregnable to the end – there was *no* fundamental relationship between art and dance. The coordinating dance tutor provided us with photographs of sculptural forms, with lengths of floating coloured materials, and with an open-ended forum for discussion; there was also the familiar medium of movement-becoming-dance, in which we could recover a feeling of security and a sense of direction. But the two-dimensional images of sculpture, and the floating chiffon, seemed worlds away from the strange 'happenings' in the art block – paint cast at random on unexpected surfaces; a lift filled with newspaper, red light, and people, going endlessly up and down; slide-making and projection on floor, walls, ceiling, bodies; little groups of people, strangely-garbed, crawling in and out of paper tents under strobe-effect lighting; the message seemed to be 'This is a dynamic experience. If it is also visual art which has elements of dance in it, it might be called a working relationship. But it is a subjective experience at all levels, different for each individual and incapable of analysis.' It was a challenge.

Later, I was able to spend a year at the Art of Movement Studio, coming to terms with principles of human movement as observed, analysed, and codified by Rudolf Laban. Movement is the raw material of dance – the medium in which

3

dance occurs. It is also the primary means by which we make sounds, and within the medium of sound music occurs. Movement also has a primary place in art, since any technique for making a visual record in whatever material – paint, clay, wood, stone, film – must begin in movement.

This understanding of movement seemed to offer a valid starting-point from which to explore not only the world of dance, but the seemingly alien world of the visual arts – so rare is it to find an artist who consciously analyses human movement; the rules of classical composition have their origins in the subjective experience of the body in space – predominently horizontal emphasis gives a feeling of calmness; vertical emphasis a feeling of dignity and aspiration; swirling lines a feeling of flow; and diagonal emphasis a feeling of lability and insecurity; beyond this, few artists seem to have recorded their deliberate use of movement ideas. Many educationalists in the art world pour scorn upon the very notion that art and dance, art and music, or art and drama can have any real interdependence. This is a record of my attempt to make a step-by-step reconnaissance into a small area of alien territory, starting from movement – the seemingly common zone between art and dance.

4

Freeing the Hands

Movement is both fundamental to human growth, and the primary means of expression. A baby thrusts and kicks with all his limbs as he experiences the new and possibly frightening sensation of undefined space all around him, where before birth there had been the warmth and security of enclosed space protecting his curled form. His cries bring about his first strong movements in the outside world, and we can guess at the effort behind them by the colour of his face and the sympathetic movements of the rest of his body. Such efforts bring about a change in his body shape, and the moving limbs come to rest in an open position where he may be content to lie for lengthening periods, though he will often return to his curled position for consolation or sleep. Sir Herbert Read (1958) writes:

The child begins to express itself from birth. It begins with certain instinctive desires which it must make known to the external world, a world which is at first represented almost exclusively by the mother. Its first cries and gestures are, therefore, a primitive language by means of which the child tries to communicate with others. But already in the first weeks of its life, we can distinguish between expression which is directed to a specific end, namely, securing the satisfaction of some appetite, such as hunger; and expression which is undirected and has no other object but to exteriorize a more generalised feeling, such as pleasure, anxiety, or anger.

During this time, the movements of the body are mainly two-sided, with the limbs thrusting impulsively and repeatedly. Two rhythms emerge – the short, staccato pattern of several successive thrusts; and the longer pattern of which this is a part – bursts of activity followed by periods of rest.

Already we may observe that the baby is moving his arms differently from his legs; the mobility of the elbow joint is greater than that of the knee, so that the arm movements are more flexible, though still impulsive and becoming stronger. He begins to grasp with his hands and gather towards his mouth, in his search for food – though he may only succeed in sucking his hand for comfort. These early hand gestures are significant; they mark a point of development in our evolutionary history which is common to all those creatures whose fore-limbs are not needed for weight-bearing, and are therefore free for more specialised activities – squirrels, sea-otters, and apes among them. The baby soon discovers that he can reach out towards an object near to him – his mother's hair, bars on the side of his cot, a toy swinging from the hood of his pram – something which is a constant and familiar part of his environment so that he begins to notice it, grasp it with his hand, and perhaps move it, or himself in relation to it. Later, another kind of arm gesture appears – pushing away, scattering, probably in distaste or anger; and different by intention from merely letting-go. Neither of these basic gestures, gathering and scattering, shows more than very rudimentary development in the feet and legs even though these limbs have no weight-bearing role, as yet; and there is far less co-ordination between the eyes and the motor activity of the lower limbs, at this stage.

Throughout this period, every main movement is accompanied by sympathetic movements in the rest of the body – the 'total bodily stir' observed and described by Laban (1963). Any attempt to confine the body inhibits these movements and may lead to some feeling of frustration, if not discomfort, in the baby during his waking hours. As he grows, he will be expected to control this 'stir' whilst he focuses his attention upon a particular body-part concerned in mastering a fine motor skill – hands above all. Such a focus of attention is very demanding, and also inhibiting; the need for alternative activities which are free, playful, and mainly physical in character, is evident in the typical free rhythm of this stage – whole-body activity, and then body-part concentration.

As yet, the baby has been concerned with exploring the area immediately around himself – his 'kinesphere' (Laban 1966) – which he will gradually extend by means of stretching and twisting movements in the body, occurring as the result of some discomfort, perhaps, or by his attempts to reach objects around him; this, in turn, leads to shifts of the body-weight, and the discovery of 'all-fours' which enables him to crawl; and sitting, which soon becomes possible without the continued grasp of the hands. Such major activities need compensating periods of recovery – though not necessarily relaxation and sleep; one kind of recovery period may be productive in quite a different way – he will lie on his back, or sit supported by a cushion, and explore his fingers and toes, gradually appreciating that they are part of himself, and that fingers particularly can do specialised work like poking or pulling at clothes or toys.

From sitting or crawling, the baby learns to pull himself upwards to explore another level than the floor – chair seats, perhaps, or the person sitting on one; he reaches towards the top rail of his cot, towards the next shelf in the cupboard, towards the inviting hands of an adult – and thus his legs and feet begin to adjust to their role of weight-bearing. He searches for a stable equilibrium in this new, vertical relationship between his centre of gravity and his feet, and when it is threatened he at first sits down, but later makes several precipitous steps before sinking suddenly or grasping something for support.

Once he has mastered his upright position, not only has he increased his mobility through taking steps instead of rolling, sliding, or crawling, but he has freed his hands from the need to support his weight, and can use them once again in the more specific ways already mentioned – with the added advantage of having more of his body-weight to reinforce such activities; pulling a box of bricks out from the bottom of the cupboard, for instance, is much more successful from a standing position than from sitting. This disposition of the body-weight has an important bearing on the quality and control of movements in any working situation; and, for the child, his present attempts to gain mastery of his body constitute a working situation.

But the significant development, at this stage, is the new freedom of the fore-limbs and the ability to grasp with the hands and direct and control their movements. Given a piece of chalk, a solid wax crayon, or any mark-making tool, and a flat area of floor, wall, or paper, he will scribble.

Making Marks

At this point in the exploration, it is relevant to study the record of observations made by Desmond Morris (1962) on the mark-making activities of young chimpanzees. Here is evidence to suggest that the first mark is made in *imitation* of some-one else's activity, rather than as a result of fortuitous accident – (perhaps a lump of chalk coming into contact with a hard, flat surface). The ape drawings and paintings collected by a number of observers show such unexpected perseverance after the initial act of imitation that one wonders why the apes have not 'stumbled upon' this mark-making activity before; could it be only because no-one has shown them how? Morris refers to a comparative study of responses made by an ape of twelve months and a child of fourteen-and-a-half months, in the Gesell writing test; to score in this test, the infant simply had to make scribble marks of any sort when offered a pencil and paper; the ape did this competently after a brief demonstration by the examiner, but the child did it for the first time spontaneously – that is, without any demonstration at all. At the next monthly test, the ape also scribbled without any prior demonstration. Allowing for the fact that apes do not find pencil, paint or even charcoal conveniently near a flat, hard, clear surface in their natural environment, to stimulate them into rather sophisticated forms of mark-making, it would seem that the spontaneous reaction of the human infant heralds the dawn of culture. Somewhere, in the remotest beginnings of prehistory, man made the first mark *spontaneously,* and then

9

imitated it: and from that time on, only imitation was strictly necessary. Yet every young child, if allowed, makes the same discovery for himself, in this and other comparable areas. Why not the apes also?

In defence of the apes, as it were, such drawing activities have been recorded as a result of the security and the association with humans that captivity implies; possibly also as a result of 'boredom' (a subjective projection) in the life of a normally active, food-gathering, territorial animal. The first two conditions bring it closer to the world of the young child; it is possible that successive generations of apes born and reared in captivity might eventually produce amongst themselves 'spontaneous artists'. Indeed, the signs are already there. W.N. and L.A. Kellogg (1933) write:

> Probably one of the most astonishing and genuinely child-like forms of non-social or self-play in which (the ape) ever indulged was to occupy herself with the moisture of her breath which had condensed upon the window-pane. She would make marks in the fogged area with the nail of her index finger and also with the end of the finger itself. Of course her tracings had no particular direction or shape; yet the very fact that she would draw them in this fashion was, in itself, it seemed to us, an unusually high type of behaviour, comparable, probably, to early scribbling in children. . .

Movement is the means by which marks are made, and at this very basic level of spontaneous mark-making the pleasing movement sensations probably motivate the early marks, and remain at least as important as the marks themselves to both ape and child for some time. But the marks have a special characteristic – they remain to be seen and considered afterwards as static records of movements, whereas movement itself is a dynamic happening – over in a moment.

The mark in the sand, on the wall, on paper is important because it gives linear shape to an otherwise diffuse sensation. The flat, two-dimensional surface imposes certain limitations, some of which might be overcome by marking the inner surface of a dome-like structure tailored to fit the reach of a child; but it is still a two-dimensional surface on which the marks appear, and therefore carries no record of movements involved in pathways across the dome. Yet the child quickly adjusts to these limitations; only when the chalk is in actual contact with the surface of the wall or paper will a mark be made; so, early scribbles tend to be continuous over an area defined by the extent of the arm gesture from a relatively fixed body-position.

Gradually, the ability to make *marks* assumes greater conscious importance than the movement sensations themselves; this is evident from the way in which a child confines himself to a small area to achieve a really 'intense' scribble; whereas a study of movement development in the young child shows such a concentration of effort to be hard-won. Why is the mark so important?

In western society, it has become common practice to provide children with the stimulus of, at least, a pencil and paper; but children find other ways of making their marks which are reminiscent of primitive and prehistoric activities – the sand-pictures of the Navaho Indians, for example (whose working methods so much influenced the young Jackson Pollock); and the hand-prints and hand-stencils of the Aurignacians (left on rock, some twenty-thousand years ago). There is the satisfaction of seeing wet foot-prints on the bathroom floor, and muddy hand-prints on the white wall; and of lying down in the snow or sand to leave behind the shape of the body. We seem to share with primitive man a need to leave our mark upon the environment – he with rock-carvings, wall-paintings, totems; we with cathedrals, landscape architecture, and dams. There is a sense of pleasure, satisfaction, even power in such achievements; and one success begets another. The marks made by the young child 'read back' or communicate to him and stimulate further marks which begin to show variety.

Given a blank sheet of paper and a satisfactory marking tool, child and ape alike will draw. If we observe the kind of movements involved, we find two factors at work – how the tool is held, and how the arm gestures affect the shapes drawn. To grip the tool in such a way that marking can be continuous requires, already, a measure of firm control; thus it is not

11

surprising to find the first tentative lines quickly becoming heavier as control increases – the tendency being to over-compensate for a 'wobbly' pencil by gripping and pressing much harder whilst binding the flow of movement. With practice, the right amount of effort is produced to achieve the desired mark; and the child has, actually at his finger-tips, a great range of possibilities – from heavy, short, straight marks all the way through to delicate, sustained, meandering lines. But such possibilities are rarely fully-explored, because the act of drawing is so soon merely a means to another end – to draw 'something'. The quality of the marking tool also will have a bearing upon the quality of the marks; Morris (1962) writes of his two-year-old chimpanzee:

> Congo put such energy and purpose into his drawing that anything meandering was somehow out of character. Only when presented with a pencil or crayon with an unfamiliar texture was he prone to meander. This occurred particularly with a very soft pencil on smooth paper.

Certain marks made by the child in the early experimental stages recur through the physical structure of the human body. The movement of the arm around the body is circular from the shoulder-joint, and mainly hinge-like at the elbow, wrist, and finger-joints. But combinations of movements across two or more of these joints give much greater mobility and increased extension, resulting in a variety of curved shapes and circles. A forward-backward movement at the wrist produces short, straight marks; a lateral movement here produces a short, opening curve which would be infinite if it could be extended; and a circular movement around this joint, achieved through the ability of the fore-arm to roll inwards and outwards produces curved lines which may become loops or circles – in any case we may consider them finite since they either meet or cross themselves; and a more complex twisting movement across wrist, elbow and shoulder produces the concave and convex curves of an S.

All these shapes have been observed in the early work of young children; they can be detected in several of the ape

droit (straight) ouvert (opening curve)

ronde (closing curve) tortille (twisted)

Fig. 1. Four fundamental trace forms

drawings; and they occur in the work of adults of primitive cultures. They begin in movement, and these movements form the basis of dance gestures also. So fundamental are they that Laban (1966) named them 'universal trace forms'. He writes:

> The tradition of the dance enumerates four fundamental trace forms which have the following shapes, called in the terminology of classical ballet 'droit' (straight), 'ouvert' (curved), 'tortille' (twisted), and 'ronde' (rounded). They are standard forms which occur in all human movements. . .and they may evolve in space in

13

one or several zones of the limbs. All trace forms can be understood as built up by these four basic formal elements. . . Form is produced by the limbs of the body and is governed by their anatomical structure which permits only certain movements to be made arising from the functions of bending, stretching, twisting, and combinations of these. This influences all writing and drawing activity of our hands and seems to restrict it to the use of the aforementioned four formal elements as a basis for shaping from which innumerable combinations can be made.

The desire to repeat a particular kind of mark, perhaps a short straight line, leads to a more conscious control of arm and hand; and movement 'patterns' within the body are established which support the identical repetition of marks, or fluency in a series of loops. Writing about ape-drawings in a general way, Morris (1962) says:

> . . . the infra-human pictures are for the most part extremely primitive. At first glance they appear to be made up of extremely simple and highly uncharacteristic short lines, with the interest lying entirely in their spatial arrangements. But a closer scrutiny reveals that whereas one chimpanzee favours short dashes another prefers long curves; where one concentrates on short, straight strokes, another makes bold, horizontal sweeps from left to right.

The illustrations in his book show the same rudimentary trace forms as in the work of young children.

Two or more marks in a certain arrangement may give extra satisfaction, so that the child or ape may try to repeat the shape he has made, and it becomes significant to him because he recognises it. One particular chimpanzee, closely observed by Morris (1962) over a period of two years, developed a radiating fan design:

> The lines of the fan were always spread out across the paper, each one being started separately at the top of the page and drawn towards the chimpanzee. The result was a highly-characteristic, roughly symmetrical, rhythmic design. In the earlier drawings it often appeared by itself, but in later sessions it was more frequently combined with curved horizontal scribbles or other markings.

Fig. 2. Brush painting by the chimpanzee Congo, showing typical radiating fan pattern. *(Coll. Mrs G.L. Carrow)*

The drawing activities of other primates show fan patterns, less clearly executed, by members of a small group of chimpanzees; and a well-defined one drawn by a Capuchin monkey on the wall of his cage.

With young children, a new factor enters at this early stage – the significant shape often acquires a name. Researchers have found that naming the shape is most often in response to some other person's enquiry; sometimes the onlooker suggests a name; sometimes the child responds to the enquiry with an apparently random naming which may be altered when another similar shape is drawn. Once the expectation has been established, every shape will be named. But even without the enquiry or suggestion from another person, naming may still occur. In a careful consideration of child art, Sir Herbert Read (1958) wrote:

> I have frequently observed that children quite spontaneously give names to their scribbles; I do not, however, find that they always subsequently discover some similarities in the scribble to justify the name. There seems to be general agreement that, at first, naming takes place after the scribble has been completed, and that only at a later stage does the child announce what his scribble is going to represent.

At this point, we might consider why a child is asked to say what his shape represents; and why, subsequently, he feels the need to name other shapes which he makes. The adult expectation is usually that drawing 'success' can best be measured by recognition of the shape drawn, whether it is 'man', 'house', or the figure 'three'. The child responds to this interest in his activities by drawing another shape, perhaps similar to the first one, perhaps not – and the naming game continues. This directs the child's attention towards sign-making, both verbal and pictorial: he learns that the speech-sound 'house' when he is out walking means a large, solid object with a special opening called 'door' and shiny patches called 'windows', where other people are sometimes seen; (his own house is usually called 'home' on such excursions); he may also learn to imitate such a shape by means of a basic pattern – a square with a triangle on top, a small rectangle inside resting on the base line, and two or more small squares roughly balanced about the rectangle – a drawing of 'house'. The adults around him seem to understand his picture, and they encourage him to develop it further – 'What did you see on the top of the house, with smoke coming out of it?' 'What are the walls made of?' Such modifications to his drawing of 'house' may enter his picture purely as pattern, in imitation of an adult device: (we are all familiar with the layers of parallel lines sectioned into 'bricks' by short, vertical, staggered lines) or he may be directed to look at houses generally with a more discriminating eye, next time he is out walking, and make his own modifications. Whatever the cause of the modification, these attempts at conscious representation open up a new channel of communication with people around him, in which the pleasure of discovery in mark-making is gradually replaced by the need for visual signs which can be understood by others.

Thus, the awareness of movement sensations associated with mark-making becomes subordinated to the required visual shape; and, through repetition, these movement patterns become part of the 'tool equipment' of the child, eventually making possible such skills as fluent handwriting, painting, paste-engraving, and any manual activity in which the continuity, consistency, and flow of movement is vital to success in achieving a further end.

Two Drawing Activities

Many careful observations of the development of children's drawings have led to classifications which vary to an extent, (less so in the early scribbles), but which are broadly in agreement with those of James Sully, a psychologist, and Ebenezer Cooke, a teacher, made almost a century ago. These classifications are summarised by Sir Cyril Burt (1921) as seven stages of development, covering the period from early childhood to adolescence. He sub-divides his first stage into four kinds of 'scribble' which he describes as follows:- 'purposeless pencillings' – the result of purely muscular movements from the shoulder, usually from right to left; 'purposive pencillings' – where the scribble itself is a centre of attention and may be given a name; 'imitative pencillings' – when the overmastering interest is still muscular, but wrist movements replace whole arm movements, and finger movements modify wrist movements, usually in an effort to imitate an older person drawing and writing; and 'localised scribbling' where the child attempts to repeat a particular shape.

A more recent classification by Rhoda Kellogg (1955) arising from a study of more than a hundred-thousand drawings and paintings produced by nursery school children, divides the early scribbles into twenty basic types – vertical, horizontal, diagonal, and curved lines; dots; zig-zags; loops; spirals; and so on. These basic scribbles combine to give six basic shapes – squares, circles, triangles, the Greek cross, diagonal crosses, and odd-shaped areas. These basic shapes are then combined or aggregated, so that a child has a graphic vocabulary to which become attached representation features – a circle 'supported' by two vertical lines is 'a man'; a circle with four (or more) radiating lines is 'a dog'; these acquire dots for eyes, more lines for hair, or a tail – the implication being that a graphic shape 'reads back' to the child, *suggesting* a particular object, and is then modified in some way to accord with his knowledge of that object; alternatively, he has the *intention* to draw a dog, and begins by drawing the circle which he remembers from previous experience but now pictures in his mind with four attached lines and two dots (the numerical accuracy is not, at this stage, significant), so that the drawing is completed in a single stage. There is an important distinction here, and we shall later see how Rudolf Arnheim takes the mind-picture of 'dog' – a circle with radiating lines – one stage further back, to the moment of perceiving the dog in actuality.

If we accept Burt's (1921) classification of early scribbles, the first two activities described by him as 'purposeless' and 'purposive' pencillings form the basis of a mainly physical activity which we may call 'kinaesthetic'; this has been analysed by Krotzsch (1917), in a work on rhythm and form in young children, and described by Read (1958) as follows:

> It arises from the pleasure a child takes in its arm movements, and in the visible traces of the movements left on the paper . . . this purely kinaesthetic activity . . . mainly a spontaneous one of muscles, the expression of an innate bodily rhythm . . . does gradually become controlled, repetitious, and consciously rhythmical. The line becomes the zig-zag, the zig-zag a wavy line, the wavy line returns on itself and become a loop, and from the loop develops the spiral and the circle.

An interruption in the rhythmical activity at this point occurs because, observers have suggested, the child suddenly

recognises the outline shape of objects in his drawing – perhaps a human face, in a circle – and from then on
he concentrates on drawing representations, no longer
concerned with pleasure in movement.

However, there are objections to this theory of sudden
recognition, and the associated idea that kinaesthetic
motivation ceases. A young child may be observed to scribble
for pleasure, and on the same occasion he may also draw
carefully a vertical line to which he adds horizontal lines on
each side and an intense scribble at the top – 'man'. When
scribbling for pleasure, the flow of his movements is relatively
free; in picture-making, the flow is bound, held back, to control
his arms and his pencil – (evident also in his breathing). If
required, he will give a name to the pleasure scribble, without
being able to show any similarity between it and the object
named. Left to himself, he may continue to scribble for
pleasure indefinitely, alongside his representational activities;
some adults fill their telephone pads with flowing and intricate
designs whilst involved in lengthy conversations.

The point should be made that a measure of kinaesthetic
awareness underlies all self-motivated drawing and painting
activity, and has much to do with the development of
technique; some artists refine their technique to a degree which
makes it impossible for the observer of the finished picture to
guess how the paint was applied to the canvas, so smooth is the
finished effect – and how well this serves the total abstraction of
Mondrian's squares, for instance; others seem to conceive a
picture from a marriage of technique with idea, so that the
flowing brush-strokes animate the landscape, the figure, or the
flower, as in the work of Matthew Smith; and sometimes the
techniques are themselves the picture, so that a record of a
sequence of movements creates its own visual form on the
canvases of Jackson Pollock.

We are concerned here with the degree of awareness of the
child or adult in the physical action of drawing or painting – a
dynamic process – as against his intention to give static form
to an image which already has a figurative definition in his
mind. Some children show kinaesthetic awareness in their

Fig. 3.   Trace forms painted by a boy aged nine immediately after a dance lesson. (Original 60 x 42 cm)

representational work, finding opportunities to indulge in trace forms which introduce a strong element of pattern into their pictures – smoke from houses and trains spiralling away into the sky; grass growing in groups of rhythmically-graded dashes; even the outline of later figure-drawings being achieved with a blend of many short, slightly curved lines instead of one deliberate unbroken delineation.

Evidence of kinaesthetic activity arising from pictorial association is shown in an example, quoted by Read (1958), of a boy of three years:

> I noticed that when cars were drawn at his request, he would sometimes take the pencil and scribble thickly and fast over the wheels. When he drew his own first cars, he would repeat this performance. What he was doing was to associate the kinaesthetic activity of scribbling with his motor image of the revolving wheels.

The pictorial language of comics – so easily understood by non-readers – appears to be based in part upon this same association; the lines of force around an exploding object, or at a point of impact, have a dynamic character as they are drawn. However, if a child employs these lines of force in his own drawings, we should not necessarily regard them as evidence of pronounced kinaesthetic awareness on his part; rather, he is probably imitating the pictorial language of schoolboy culture, so that his pencil is less informed by the immediate pleasurable sensation than by his memory – he recalls an earlier visual image of a 'bang!' and this he draws. The true kinaesthetic artist works in the immediate situation of movement awareness and his painting is, in part, a voyage of discovery in uncharted seas – he must make his own records of movement as he paints, and anything recalled from memory will be recalled by means of the particular gestural experience arising from movement sensations.

Jean Piaget (1970) distinguishes between static images, which are straightforward reproductions of objects perceived at the moment of drawing or recalled from memory; and anticipatory images, which require the ability to think creatively, to propose new changes, to grasp the nature of

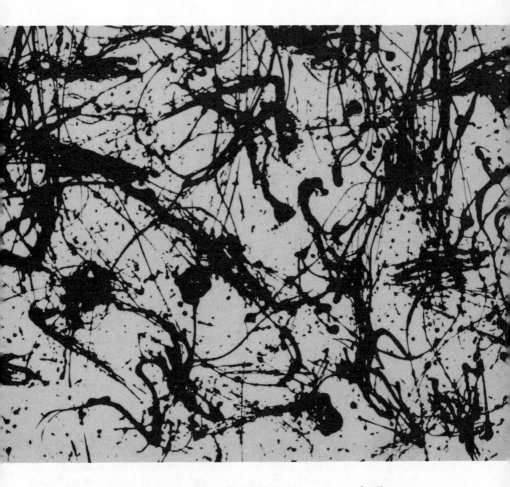

Fig. 4. 'Number thirty-two' by Jackson Pollock. (Black duco on canvas; detail approx 150 x 230 cm from original 265 x 460 cm)

movement. The schoolboy who uses the 'bang' signs may recall a static, reproductive image from newspaper comic strips; whereas the inventor of the 'balloon' device, whereby characters are shown speaking, allowed the physiological experience of breathing to influence the necessity for dialogue – resulting in an anticipatory image which could be expressed graphically. The artist whose awareness of the gestural movements available to him already affects his visual image of a landscape *at the moment of looking* will have a different mental image from the artist who registers the formal elements of the proposed composition; but both will make use of a reproductive image of the landscape. If, however, one of them proposes to himself the notion that he might translate a particular experience of, say, aggressive and violent activity – a dynamic event – into a graphic illustration, he will require an anticipatory image; it may be fully formed before he begins to paint, or it may grow and change as the painting develops.

Where divergence between two drawing and painting activities clearly occurs, it is the result of distinct intentions on the part of the child who is drawing. On the one hand, there is the satisfaction to be gained from transferring inner sensations – himself – to the outer world of marks on paper; on the other, there is the attempt to record his view of an object which he sees (or has seen) in the external world; his view of that object will develop with increasing visual awareness, and details and complexities will be accommodated in each successive drawing attempt. But the kinaesthetic drawing activity is mainly a matter of assimilating familiar 'skills' playing with things already experienced in these early years; if an interesting shape or pattern arises, and there is an attempt to copy it, the second drawing is more likely to be achieved by painstaking effort to imitate *what he sees in front of him,* than by recalling the movement sensations that gave rise to the original shape; and the copy is unlikely to be 'successful' because it will not be informed with the same quality of kinaesthetic awareness that was present in the original.

There is evidence to suggest that some children continue to

perceive life through 'kinaesthetic eyes' almost entirely. Observations of the work of partially-sighted and blind children, whose visual perception was severely limited or lacking from birth, were used as the basis for studies of normal children; and these studies demonstrated that all children have strong tendencies towards one or other of two types – named by Viktor Lowenfeld (1964) as *visual* and *haptic*. To quote Read (1958) on this distinction:

> The visual type starts from his environment, and his concepts are developed into a perceptual whole through the fusion of partial visual experiences – (that is) a visual representation is not necessarily an instantaneous impressionistic apprehension of form from one fixed point of view; it may be the translation into concrete, plastic form of a visual concept – the synthesis of many points of view.

(We shall see later that Arnheim (1966) proposes 'spontaneous pure forms of sensory perception' which would invalidate Read's idea of a synthesis occurring at all; but this does not affect the notion of two types.)

> The haptic type, on the other hand, is primarily concerned with his own bodily sensations and with the actual space around him. The haptic artist is primarily concerned, not with an object in the outer world, but with his own inner world of sensation and feeling. Such a type is not necessarily blind or weak-sighted; he merely does not use his eyes. The further optical experience recedes into the background the less important does the eye become as the intermediary of the concept. To the same extent, the importance of the environment diminishes and experience is more and more confined to the processes that go on in the body as a whole, bodily sensations, muscular innervations, deep sensibilities, and their various emotional effects.

Read goes on to say that the sense of touch becomes the intermediary between these inner sensations and the concept; and it is easy to see how pain and heat, for instance, which must have influenced his remarkable example of 'Earache' painted by a girl of thirteen, were conveyed through a sense of touch;

her concept was that earache occupied half her head and inflated her ear to a monstrous size. No visual model could have conveyed this experience.

Lowenfeld (1964) himself writes:

> The visual-haptic theory is important to understand, for it underlies much development in art. Young children's art can be generally classified as haptic in nature, for the experiences portrayed are those that originate primarily with the self, and include what might be considered touch-space. The increasing visual awareness of children can be seen in their drawings and paintings... For some, the emphasis on visual representation can become a burden with which they are not able to deal, and art for the haptically-minded individual may in some cases be a frustrating experience. The rewards in the elementary school may have gone to those children who were the most visually-aware of their environment. The teacher in the secondary school may be confronted with children who have rejected the world of visual art and decided, therefore, that they cannot draw or paint. The haptic art that can be elicited from such children whose expression has been previously thwarted is often emotionally-charged and full of released expression.

It is debatable whether or not the haptic child is the same as the child who is kinaesthetically-aware – the one would seem to be concerned with bodily states, which may indeed give rise to images capable of graphic expression, but *static* images, most probably; the other with *changes* of state, with movement, which the child can only express *in movement* (though the resulting patterns or pictures may be equally pleasing as graphic images – a record of many dynamic experiences, captured in static form). But, clearly, they both belong in adjacent areas for study purposes by reason of the internal stimulus for their imagery; whereas the child whose stimulus for imagery originates in the environment is drawing and painting with a different motive.

To summarise:- we have the young child, drawing and painting for pleasure in the activity itself; and also, with rather more deliberation, drawing and painting representations of

Fig. 5. Trace forms painted by a boy aged nine immediately after a dance lesson. (Original 60 x 42 cm)

objects in the world around him. In many children, this second activity may entirely replace the first; or the first may be partially-recalled in attempts to imitate the motion of wheels and the spiralling of smoke; or in the fluency of writing patterns; or in 'doodling' at times of preoccupation. Parallel with this, but not to be confused with it, is the tendency of some children to find a source of imagery within themselves arising from inner sensations which may appear to distort their visual perception – (that is to say, haptic imagery, translated into the visual medium of drawing and painting may appear distorted and puzzling *to the observer*). Inner sensations of which the child is aware, but which are transitory because they arise in the dynamic experiences of movement, also give rise to imagery, but this imagery is of such a fleeting kind that it is unlikely to be used consciously by any young child – though we may see evidence of its influence in the *quality* of scribbles, patterns, and brush-strokes in picture-making; in heavy, short, straight lines or light, continuous, meandering lines, for instance. This kinaesthetic drawing activity may well evolve from the earlier 'scribbling for pleasure'; if not, there is the possibility that it may be developed with guidance, as an alternative source of imagery linked with movement education generally, and having a bearing upon manual and gestural techniques in particular.

Kinaesthetic
Motivation

Before looking more closely at the further development of kinaesthetic activity in drawing and painting, there should be some consideration of the conclusions reached by Desmond Morris (1962) as a result of his study of infra-human art. His approach was made with the intention of throwing more light upon the aesthetic factor in art and how early in evolutionary development its influence might be detected. Without moving too far into the field of aesthetics, it is clear that 'kinaesthetic activity' must belong, in part, to this area. If we accept its name at face value, implying 'pleasure in moving' (or, more precisely, the performance and perception of movements of 'felt' interest), it should be possible to deduce the existence of this in infra-human art by the willingness of apes and monkeys to scribble 'for fun'.

By offering his chimpanzees only paper and pencil or paintbrush, and no inducements in the way of rewards to motivate them, he was able to confirm that drawing is a self-rewarding activity, in the same category as play, curiosity, self-expression and investigation. He says:

> Most of (these self-rewarding activities) are basically physical, motoric outbursts and are fundamentally similar to human gymnastics and sports, except that they lack any ulterior motives such as the obtaining of health, money, or social standing. They

29

may inadvertently keep the animal mentally and physically healthy and thus indirectly assist it in its struggle for survival, but the actual driving-force behind these self-rewarding activities appears to be simply the unleashing of surplus nervous energy. In this connection, it is noticeable that it is just those species which are particularly active when they are faced with life's usual survival problems, that are also especially prone to perform self-rewarding activities when everything is taken care of for them.

In order to investigate ape paintings as objectively as possible, Morris (1962) separated the picture contents into what he saw as their two basic elements – composition and calligraphy. By composition he meant the nature of the spatial relationships between the units of a picture; and by calligraphy he meant the nature of each individual unit taken by itself.

He found evidence of compositional control – that is, an ability to 'manage' the space on the paper in such a way that not only were the marks confined to the paper, but they were arranged in certain ways too deliberate and recurring to be dismissed as accidental. One chimpanzee marked each corner of the paper with great care before making use of the central space; when presented with a sheet of paper on which a simple, but incomplete, pattern was already drawn, she 'completed' the pattern; and if the given pattern was off-centre, she balanced it by scribbling in a complementary area. Although the completion tests and the balancing tests are very important in establishing the visual control of the ape, they do introduce an external factor which focuses her attention and therefore modifies her intention, so that the kinaesthetic activity is already subordinated to an external requirement – as when children are given an outline picture to colour in. One may argue that, merely by putting a sheet of paper in front of the ape or child, one is already controlling the kinaesthetic activity, by limiting the working space; for this reason, it would be interesting to compare their drawing activities on larger, perhaps undefined areas – certainly large enough to accommodate a fully-extended gesture of the arm from a fixed working position, since this position is important if the picture is to have any visual relationship with the kinaesthetic awareness of equilibrium about a central axis, and the centre of gravity. However, the ape drawings on blank sheets of paper provide a fascinating field for the study of visual compositions arising from kinaesthetic activity.

Calligraphy is defined in the dictionary as 'beautiful handwriting'. We must assume that it can have a more general meaning – such as the careful formation of the simplest individual units, such as those early marks made by apes and young children; these are the basic material of later organised visual compositions, as letters are the basic material of written words and sentences. By using the Kellogg classification of early scribble types, Morris (1962) was able to compare the development of ape drawings with those of young children, using the young male chimpanzee Congo as his main subject. He writes:

> . . . it is clear (that) in many ways Congo and the human children had very similar scribble responses. It seems likely that the differences between them at this stage were due to the differences in muscular development, rather than to any differences in mental processes. The fact that Congo was *composing* his pictures in a better way during his earlier phases is undoubtedly due to the same muscular differences. For, by the time children have sufficient control over their pencils, their brains are already at that stage which is dominated by calligraphic variation and invention.

The Kellogg classification then moves on to a consideration of diagrams and aggregates. Morris (1962) discusses the emergence and development of Congo's most characteristic aggregate – the fan pattern – in his chapter on compositional control. The fan pattern appeared in over ninety of almost four hundred pictures made by Congo, and is discussed at length by Morris:

> The number of lines that made up a fan pattern varied between forty and six, and it was noticeable that the fans with the largest number of lines were usually those drawn with thin pencil points, whereas those made using a thick paint-brush usually had far fewer

31

lines . . . the angles of the lines and the relationships of these angles to the positions of the lines were analysed, and it was found that, in many cases, if the fan was projected downwards, the lines would meet at a point that was approximately the centre of the chimpanzee's body, as it sat at its picture-making. This fact, combined with the observation that each of the fan-pattern lines was started at the top of the page and progressed towards the animal, immediately suggested a possible biological significance for the pattern. If a young chimpanzee is given a loose mass of bedding material, such as straw or hay, it will sit in the centre of it and then gather in towards its body handful after handful until it has a circular bed, or nest, packed tight around its body. . . This bed-making routine has several points of similarity with the drawing of a fan pattern. In the first place, the arm goes through a similar series of stretches and bends in each instance. . . In both cases the movements are radially arranged and in both cases there is a visual feed-back controlling the degree of displacement from movement to movement . . . it was sometimes observed that Congo would stop . . . and might then continue, and complete the pattern using the other hand . . . there is a predisposition for this type of rhythmic response already built into the chimpanzee system that favours the production of this type of pattern.

(But) . . . the creation of a perfect fan pattern by a Capuchin monkey (on the vertical wall of his den) can be cited as giving a wider significance to the action . . . another possible explanation of the fan pattern phenomenon (is) the theory of 'mechanical simplicity'. . . Using this approach it might be argued that Congo and the Capuchin and the other fan pattern makers were only using the simplest mechanical movements of their arms to fill the space in front of them . . . the selection of this particular pattern by both capuchin and chimpanzee, does give some weight to the argument that motoric simplicity may be the controlling factor.

As a piece of pure movement study, 'gathering' towards the centre of the body allows for firm, direct control over the action; and recalling that the first clearly-defined gestures of the human baby are of gathering in towards himself, it is perhaps not surprising that in an activity like drawing, which requires

Fig. 6. Painting by a chimpanzee showing split fan pattern with central blob.
(Desmond Morris)

above all that the marking tool should remain in contact with the surface, we should see the first deliberate pattern growing from a fundamental movement activity in which control can not only be maintained, but increased. The radial lines which make up the fan pattern are reminiscent of gestural pathways in the forward zone of the body – easier to achieve and therefore more familiar. However, the Capuchin's vertical fan is not to be accounted for in quite this way, and may have more to do with his feeling for stability; he is shown crouching in front of his fan pattern, but in order to begin each of the lines at its outermost point, he would need to reach up and thus lift his centre of gravity a little way from the ground; and control over each line would be most easily achieved as he returned to the crouching position. Perhaps, after all, it is simply a matter of the centre of the fan occurring at the point of greatest security – where the marked surface is in closest proximity to the anchored centre of gravity, whether of crouching Capuchin or seated ape. But mechanical simplicity and physical laws alone will not explain why each gesture should extend outwards to a different point before brush or pencil begin the next radial line; this must be in response to a visual demand.

Here we have the emergence of a clearly-recognisable form in art, arising from kinaesthetic activity, and capable of repetition; this form is evidently important to the ape; and Morris (1962) was satisfied that it was a fixed visual unit – that is, a form accompanied by a mental image – as a result of two particular instances; he writes:

The creation of the reverse fan was one of those moments of pure creativeness, where the experimenter could hardly believe his eyes. As I have said, Congo produced over ninety fan patterns, always starting each line at its far point and drawing it towards himself. On the day in question, Congo had drawn several fan patterns in the usual way and then, as the next blank card was placed in front of him, a strange intensity seemed to overtake him and, with soft, almost inaudible grunts, he began laboriously to make a fan, starting each line at a near and central point and spreading it away from him. As each line was marked out, he could be seen carefully

Fig. 7. Painting by chimpanzee Congo, showing a subsidiary fan motif. *(Coll. Donald Harker)*

studying its course, so that it radiated away in a fresh direction from those already made. The fan was therefore similar in appearance to any normally-produced one, but had been drawn completely in reverse. This astonishing performance can only be explained if one assumes that Congo had reached the stage where he had a *fan image* in his brain and that he was virtually experimenting with a new way of producing it. The subsidiary fan example gives further proof of this. In this picture, Congo had already painted a rather ineffectual main fan and then towards the end of the picture, took a brush of black paint and quite deliberately, with five rhythmically-delivered strokes, formed a perfect, small, off-centre, subsidiary fan shape. The focal point is not only to one side of the picture, but it is also within the area of the picture and does not therefore correspond with the position of the animal's body.

If we dare to generalise from the particular, it would seem that the emergence of a fixed visual unit, whether in apes or children, marks a developmental stage at which all drawing stimuli may arise externally, unless there is some encouragement to continue searching within oneself – consciously – for the kinaesthetic motivation which shapes the external forms.

Images in Drawing

From such studies it begins to be clear that the mainly exploratory activities of the child undergo a change when the motivation for drawing is no longer that of pleasurable sensation in the action itself, but satisfaction in the look of the drawing completed. This would seem to suggest that the child sets himself a task beforehand and works until it is finished – using 'beforehand' in the very specific sense of the moment before any particular line is added to the paper, and 'finished' in the same specific sense. Observations of a child at this early age suggest that a composition grows as a result of several successive ideas, rather than one main idea sustained throughout several minutes of concentration: (using 'composition' to mean the total number of units scattered about the paper, rather than any one area of concentrated activity). But, clearly, the idea precedes the action, if only by the fraction of a second, and a probable development of this process is that a single idea should be more complex in its first formulation in the child's mind proportionately as the child becomes more able to sustain that complex idea throughout the time it takes to complete the drawing. However, it is important to distinguish between the complexities which were already present in his original idea, and which he will want to include in his picture before he feels that it is finished, and later apparent complexities which he may add through adult

37

prompting, or as space-filling devices – and not because they were present in his original image.

'Idea' carries within its meaning a suggestion of thought processes at work, as though certain mental activities are necessary before even a simple line can be added to the paper; 'image' conveys a mental picture of a line, two lines crossing, a pattern of lines, or a picture – something instantaneous which arises in the mind as a result of a stimulus, and not as a result of working thoughts. The extensive researches of Jean Piaget (1970) and his associates have led them to the conclusion that working thoughts – 'operational thought' – will not normally occur until the age of seven or eight, although preparations for this development are a part of the 'pre-operational' stage. It is therefore more relevant to speak of 'images' in connection with the early drawing activities of the young child.

In attempting to trace the nature and the source of a young child's images, we have to turn to psychology, since observation alone cannot supply the answers. We are told that the subject – a sensitive human being, a living organism equipped with several senses – is able to use these senses to apprehend objects which are mainly separate and external from him, and part of his environment with which he must come to terms in order to survive. The young child, on holiday at the sea-side, looks at the sea – a vast, flat, grey or blue space; he feels the wetness of the water, he tastes its saltiness, he hears the rush of pebbles under the tide, he smells the sea-weed on the tide-line; all this is in his perception of the sea, though perhaps none of it is clearly differentiated; and with it, he may be acutely aware of the movement and pressure of the water as he paddles, or is carried by his father into deeper water to practise swimming.

At home, he sees his father's car parked in front of the house; he hears it roar into throbbing 'life', and smells petrol and exhaust fumes; he can climb in and out of the car and grasp and press a variety of objects associated with the dashboard; the outside of the car is hard and smooth to touch and may leave dust on his fingers. All these experiences make up his general idea of CAR. Out in the street he can see other objects which look, sound, and smell like CAR; they have enough about them that is familiar to be associated with the car in the garden. His book has pictures of objects which, though small, look a little like his father's car – but he hears only the speech-sound 'car' made by his mother, not the roar of the engine; he feels the flat, shiny, pliable surface of paper, not the curved, rigid surface of the metal body; he smells paper and print, not exhaust fumes and petrol; and he certainly cannot get inside the pictured car. Yet something about it corresponds with his experiences, and he recognises it as A CAR. If he later attempts to *draw* a car, his drawing will correspond with an image present in his mind at the time of drawing – whether or not he can see a car through the window, or in his picture book – an image formed according to his awareness of characteristics common to the appearance of cars in general; what we might call 'car-ness'. Rudolf Arnheim (1966) writes upon the subject of 'roundness':

A child draws a human head as a circle. This is not an attempt to reproduce the specific outline of a particular person's head but rather a general form quality of a head, of heads in general – namely, roundness . . . the child's circle . . . is an image, a generally-accepted image of that roundness common to the shape of heads . . . it is a representation that eliminates many of the perceptual characteristics of heads and limits itself to a form that renders the structure of roundness in a pure, clear-cut way. . .

If this theory is acceptable, the elementary processes of perception, far from being mere passive registration, are creative acts of grasping structure, even beyond the mere grouping and selecting of parts. What happens in perception is similar to what, at a higher psychological level is described as understanding or insight. Perceiving is abstracting, in that it represents individual cases through configurations of general categories.

So we understand that the child does not recall many images of cars seen on different occasions from many angles (including the car in his picture book) in order to synthesise all these impressions into one image which he then draws; but rather that each moment of awareness of CAR – each act of perception – carries in it the recognition of some common visual characteristic by which any car is known; and this he will draw. It is as though the child, confronted with a jumble of potential stimuli – a vague and undifferentiated neutral 'otherness' against which he himself is only partially delineated by means of sensation – becomes aware of particular things around him through the relevant sense organs and his own innate ability to grasp basic structures, or patterns composed of those structures.

We must now consider how he transfers what he has perceived to paper. It is necessary to note that 'what he has perceived' does not mean 'what he has seen'; his retina could be shown to have recorded everything which another child or an adult had recorded at the same moment, but his perception is predisposed to 'notice' only certain things; and it is these certain things which combine to make his mental image. According to Paul Guillaume (1971), and Piaget (1951), imitation is a vital element in the learning process, (and not a mindless, mechanical activity which bespeaks a lack of originality); the visual perception of the car is not an instantaneous camera picture, but a relatively lengthy and painstaking process on the part of the eyes which 'follow' the main features of the car and enable them to be recorded in the mind as a mental image; thus the eyes imitate the car (as the child perceives it). Next, there must be active imitation of the mental image before any drawing of CAR can begin to take shape; the child 'looks at' the picture in his mind, 'follows' its outlines, 'sees' it in terms of what his pencil will do – all this in active preparation for each moment of drawing, each gestural movement, which will produce the components of the graphic image on paper; concrete, external, fixed, and capable of imitation by others (or further imitation by himself), whereas the child's own mental image was internal, transient, and available only to himself. The process of translating mind into matter requires the vital, intermediate stage of gesture – here, a *utilitarian* activity made up of several movements which imitate the structure of the mental image.

Piaget and Inhelder (1970) tell us that these gestures are simpler than the internalized mental image, and it is clear that one kind of gesture – a closing curve, for example – can be adapted to imitate several parts of the image of CAR. These gestures in themselves bear evidence of basic structure, of form quality, as Laban (1966) observed; and each gesture has to be selected by the child and adapted to the two-dimensional situation in order that the pencil should make contact with the paper and leave a fixed graphic image. The selection and adaptation may well bring about some modification of the original mental image, and the temptation is to believe that all the drawings of young children are somehow poor reproductions of what is in the mind. But we should be careful to distinguish between the rudimentary visual percept of CAR in terms of, perhaps, a large circular shape (the body) with smaller circular shapes (wheels) intersecting its circumference; and circular shapes poorly-executed through inadequate gestural control; both drawings show some recognition of the inherent visual structure of cars in general, but only the second could be called a poor reproduction.

We are all able to perceive external objects, like the sea, and a car, alongside the child; and our percepts, though not the same, will bear similar characteristics because our senses are similarly stimulated. We usually discriminate between the sensations aroused in us as we wade into the sea – coldness and wetness, saltiness, tanginess, pressure and lift, and the sight of endless ocean ahead of us; even when the total sensory experience is so exciting that discrimination is blurred (the probable condition of the child) we ourselves are aware of some associated imagery – particularly if we hear in terms of pitch and volume, or see in terms of colour and mass; we may later re-create those images, with instrumentation, or with paint and canvas. Yet it is unlikely that such images will be quite free of the associated sensations of the original experience, though we shall only be able to imitate those characteristics belonging to our chosen medium. Outstanding among the visual characteristics may be the immense space across the surface of the sea which we apprehend by means of reference points – a boat, another person, a curling wave-crest in the foreground. It is perhaps not surprising that a young child, attempting to recall his image of the sea at the request of an adult, draws only the associated objects like sand-castles, boats, and shells, and seems to omit the sea altogether; it defies his apprehension of shape, pattern, order, visual structure (as indeed it does for many adults also); and he cannot replace the missing image by thought processes as an older child might do. Yet we cannot assume from the evidence of his picture that he did not notice the sea at all; like ourselves, he will have been aware of several sensations (which we can deduce from his reactions at the time of the experience) – foremost among them, perhaps, the sensation of movement which arises from two situations; the resistance of the legs and body to the ebb and flow of the tide when attempting to wade into the sea; and the lift and suspension of buoyancy which comes with confidence in the new element.

If these are familiar sensations, associated with his every view of the sea, we may expect his view – his visual percept – to be shaped accordingly. He may not succeed in evolving a 'drawing' image of the rhythmically-moving sea for himself, but he may be happy to imitate another's image; the conventional symbol for SEA is a wavy line with points uppermost, or several parallel wavy lines; like the lines of 'explosion' in comics, some children will simply imitate the graphic sign as a device or code; but most are happy to accept its simple and regular pattern because it corresponds with their 'feelings' about the sea which is not yet reasoned thought; and variations on the simple wavy line show some attempt to align the feeling with developing visual perception; or, put another way, what we see is the child's attempt to select the only obvious visual characteristic of his mainly tactile-kinaesthetic awareness of the sea which may be drawn – and that is the linear definition of the surface, the wavy line.

If an older child, in an attempt to paint the sea itself as object, is also unable or unwilling to dissociate entirely his visual percept from other awarenesses of sea, the result may be a picture which at first compares strangely with our own visual percepts. The rhythmic movement of the water may be conveyed in a pattern of sustained, heavy/light markings covering the entire paper, with no attempt to delineate the

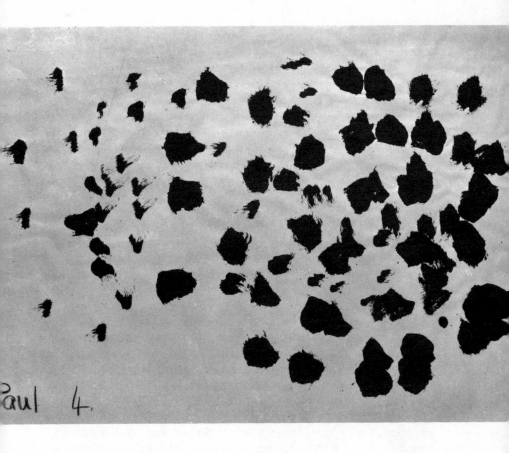

Fig. 8.   Firm and light patterns painted by a boy aged four immediately after dance lessons. (Original 60 x 42 cm)

surface of the sea. The immediate visual communication of such a picture is unfamiliar when our expectations are conditioned to the more traditional 'view'; and it is necessary to enter into the 'feeling' of the picture in order to understand it.

If we are prepared to approach such a picture of the sea in this way, we may also look at early scribbles, and at later developments arising from them, from the same point of view – as pictures of a child's feelings about *himself* moving smoothly or jerkily in roundabout ways or straight lines, heavily or lightly, slowly or quickly; and we may regard this both as a means of expression and a development of technique; looked at in this light, such activity may be further extended, by encouraging him to experience and control an increasing range of kinaesthetic sensations which, in turn, bring about a greater variety of 'free' patterns through the activity of the gesturing arm.

Whether or not the earliest scribbles are accompanied by even the most rudimentary visual images, there can be no doubt about the young child's pleasure in relatively uninhibited movement which leaves marks behind; and the deliberate use of heavy/light, slow/sudden, wavy/straight marks indicates the presence of kinaesthetic awareness; if this can be recalled by the child in his gestural action without the necessity of a model to imitate (another person pressing, or stroking, or snaking across the paper) we are entitled to deduce the presence of *kinaesthetic imagery*. But if a model is necessary, or if there is an attempt to reproduce a particular kind of mark by *visual imitation* of that mark, the awareness is concentrated upon the *look* of the action or the *look of the end result*, rather than upon the special *manner* of achieving it.

Here it is necessary to refer again to Piaget and Inhelder's (1970) researches on mental imagery in the child. They classify images according to their structure – a basic division into *reproductive images*, evoking objects or events already known; and *anticipatory images* which, by figural imagination, represent events (movements, transformations, or their culmination or results) that have not previously been perceived. In the context of drawing activity, we may assume

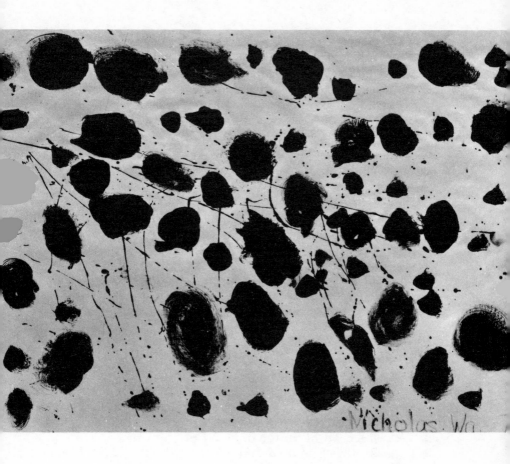

Fig. 9.   Firm and light patterns painted by a boy aged seven immediately after dance lessons. (Original 60 x 42 cm)

that 'purposeless pencillings' (Burt 1921) in the earliest scribble stage are not accompanied by visual imagery; but when the scribble itself is a centre of attention, some areas of significance may emerge as rudimentary visual images in the mind; and in 'localised scribbling' (Burt 1921) these significant areas or marks can be reproduced by the child through the intervention of a series of static images. But the child is, as yet, unable to *imagine* shapes to draw that have not already been perceived externally by him, either in the visual feedback of his own scribbles, or in imitation of someone else's drawing, or as an object in his environment.

However, the scribble period contains also a stage of 'imitative pencillings' (Burt 1921) in which the child's attention is less upon the marks occurring on the paper, and more upon the actions of his arm, wrist, and fingers – *imitating the action* of an adult rather than the resulting graphic form on paper. To copy an action, he will formulate another set of visual images – each one static, but also part of a sequence representing the adult's movements. The action is repeated, and the movement sensations are 'recorded' in the body – having, by now, less to do with the look of an action and more to do with its feel. Eventually, the feel of an action will replace its look entirely, thus enabling the body to develop a motor skill; and allowing for concentration upon the visual images which build up the drawing or painting.

Thus far, the child draws only what he feels, or what he has actually seen – whether he sees it in front of him as simple marks on the paper or interesting shapes arising out of a chance combination of marks, which he then imitates; or sees it in his mind as a visual memory image from previous drawing activities; or abstracts from life 'roundness' of heads and 'verticality' of legs for his first drawings of MAN. These sources of imagery will carry him well beyond the scribble stage (as defined by Burt) through schematic drawings of the human figure, a house, a car, 'catalogues' of people or objects, repetitive pattern-making, and signs for letters and numbers – all made possible through imitation of *static reproductive images*. Yet already the ground is being prepared for the emergence of anticipatory images – those representing movements, transformations, or their culmination or results, that have not previously been perceived and cannot therefore be imitated; in other words, for a particular work of the imagination which depends upon operational thought. (Piaget and Inhelder (1970) chose to test this ability by asking children to picture the result of cutting corners from a sheet of paper folded three times and then opened out.)

This preparation for anticipatory images occurs in the *intermediate stage* mentioned in connection with the act of imitation; the child perceives a dog, perhaps; this visual perception involves movements of the eyes which follow the main 'pattern' of the dog – however simple this pattern – to build a mental image of DOGNESS; this mental image is delineated in *gestural movements* which give the graphic image of DOG on paper. But although the eyes can imitate the dog image, simply to familiarize it, the executional gestures necessary to carry out the drawing have no action model to follow and must assemble the necessary motor skills from a medley of past experiences. Even when the child is looking at the dog (or at his memory image of a dog) with the intention of drawing it – that is, when his visual percept is of 'drawn dog' – he has already made use of *anticipatory executional gestures* in his seeing. Thus, however vague and fleeting are these intermediate images which anticipate successful movements for drawing a dog, they are the beginnings of the anticipatory images associated with operational thought; and this is a stage in the development of the child which usually occurs around the age of seven to eight years, according to Piaget.

Once a child has reached this stage, he is able to anticipate events and results which have not formerly been an exact part of his experience, and the whole thinking process takes a great step forward. The anticipatory images which accompany this kind of thinking are of two sorts; they either picture the result of a change (the chair in a new position; the folded paper open to show all the holes); or else they picture the changes at successive stages (the chair lifted, held, lowered; the paper unfolded once, twice, three times). It is easier to imagine the results than the changes which bring them about; but the desire to achieve a particular result is usually sufficient motivation for the imagery of the intervening stage. We should note that Piaget and Inhelder (1970) make an interesting exception to this difficulty in imagining changes – where the stages of a change have to do with the activity of the child's own body, rather than with alterations to external objects; at the time of writing this text, the conclusions of their research into this particular area of imagery were not available; but from observation it is clear that suggestions like 'Make a big, wide shape', 'Curl up small', 'Twist round in your chair' present no difficulties in the immediate pre-operational stage.

The presence of visual imagery in thinking and in drawing makes possible the conscious use of percepts which occur in the present – 'I'm going to draw you'; those which are recalled from the past – 'This is Granny's house . . . when can I give it to her?' and those which are imagined 'This is my monster!' We should now consider what imagery, if any, arises in movement which is not serving the cause of drawing – (that is, movement not in its utilitarian role of anticipatory executional gestures) – and which is not stimulating drawing activity in a prolonged 'dialogue' in the scribble stage. In other words, we need to know what kind of image might be present in the mind of the moving child who has no intention to draw, but whose interest in moving may lead him to dance.

Images in Movement

All human movement has a purpose. It may be to relieve physical discomfort, as in stretching after a period of confined sitting; it may be to alter the relationship of an object with its environment, such as moving a chair, or oneself from A to B; it may be to communicate, as in beckoning or nodding; or to express a raw emotion, such as anger or desire; it may be to move for the pleasure of moving, whether in the mastery of skills for games and sports or the rhythmic steps and symbolic gestures of dance.

If we begin with the baby, we find movements occurring in response to physiological stimuli, such as pain or hunger; or external stimuli, like a sudden sound; – reflex actions without (we think) conscious awareness of the movements themselves. So the question of mental imagery does not arise. We also find movements expressing emotions of anger, or unhappiness, when an overwhelming feeling cannot be contained, and body, limbs, and vocal chords are one in violent or prolonged activity – the kicking, heel-drumming, back-arching tantrum; the reaching upward or forward after the departing mother, and the sobbing appeal – any mental imagery here would picture only the object of the baby's anger or unhappiness; he is, as yet, unaware of the expressive power of his movements, because they are spontaneous rather than deliberate (Arnheim, 1956)–*'physiognomic'* rather than *'descriptive'*–and therefore

49

not yet a language, but only signs to the sensitive observer. But the feeling-states of excitement, and contentment, may bring about the beginning of movement awareness – the result, perhaps, of incidental sounds occurring as the excited baby kicks or bangs the tray of his high chair; so, he repeats the activity; or of incidental sights when the hands of the contented baby make a 'fingerplay' in front of his eyes, and he prolongs the activity; in both instances, he imitates his own activity because he enjoys the results. In becoming aware of cause and effect, the baby or the young child relies as much upon tactile-kinaesthetic experience as upon aural or visual experience. In this context, Michotte is quoted by Piaget and Inhelder (1970):

> . . . visual perception of causality derives, by means of assimilation, from the tactile-kinaesthetic perception of causality. It is in fact probable that a large number of perceptual structurations in the child are elaborated within a context of progressive coordination of the tactile-kinaesthetic and visual ranges . . . and it is only later that vision becomes completely independent, after a whole legacy of tactile-kinaesthetic experience has been acquired.

This leads us to suppose that some kind of imagery accompanies any movements made deliberately by the child, though the earliest images will most probably picture the results of movements, rather than the movements themselves. From observation of a toddler with his teddy-bear, we can deduce three stages relevant to this study in the process of transferring the toy from the cupboard to a chair; first, he takes the toy from the cupboard; holding it tightly, he moves rather uncertainly about the room with it; then he staggers against the chair, and suddenly places the toy in the chair with the air of one who recognises the rightness of the placing – he has seen it there before! For the teddy-bear on the shelf he needed only visual perception; the act of picking it up and holding it belongs to the early, instinctive gathering-in movements, needing no visual imagery but only a tactile-kinaesthetic awareness, retained whilst he moves about the room; the fortuitous juxtaposition of teddy-bear and chair seems to recall a happy association which he consolidates by his action. Nothing in all this has demanded of him any forethought.

An older child would accomplish the task by a different process. His intention, from the beginning, is to place the toy in the chair, where he has seen it before. He already has an image in his mind of the toy in that position; and he has a visual percept of the toy in its present position on the cupboard shelf. He sees himself holding it, he visualises walking from the cupboard to the chair, and the task is as good as accomplished *in his mind* even before he begins to move, with the help of two images – one static, reproductive image (the toy in the chair) recalled from memory, and one anticipatory executional image proposing the means of transfer (himself carrying the toy across the room). Of course, the means of transfer may prove unsuccessful in the event, but he *visualises* himself doing it.

A third child might approach the problem in another way. He might decide to move the chair to the cupboard before lifting down the toy. He recalls seeing his mother lift the chair and move it to another position, though not next to the cupboard; but he has an anticipatory image of the chair in that position, and he will imitate the recalled image of his mother lifting it. He *visualises* the problem as solved. But when he attempts to pick up the chair, it is too heavy for him to lift and carry. In the process of trying to lift it, he feels it slide; so he slides it across the floor to the cupboard, and places the toy in it. The incidental sliding movement is a new piece of experience which he deliberately uses by imitating himself applying force to cause the chair to move. The original anticipatory image has provided the motivation for solving the problem through experience, through trial and error, when the recalled visual image of the executional model (his mother lifting the chair) has failed him.

But according to Piaget and Inhelder (1970), the child's image of himself walking across the room, or pushing the chair, is not an image of continual movement, but rather a series of 'cinematographic stills' which show various key positions in the process – certainly a starting position and an ending, maybe several points on the way:

51

Try, for instance, imagining a cyclist's leg movements. One can visualise slight displacements as a foot goes down, round, and up again. But one thinks one has got the continuity only to realise that one has prolonged the image *in thought,* and that one is no longer actually 'seeing' the whole in motion. . . The inability of the *image* to apprehend a kinetic continuum likewise has nothing to do with perception, since *perception of movement* can be very subtle. . . The static character of the image . . . can only be due to the exigencies of figural representation. And it is interesting to find that here also there is a link between the graphic image and the strictly mental image.

So visual images relating to movement can only show positions along the way, and thought must provide the continuity.

However, if we become the cyclist, poised ready for action, the images will be different. We are no longer aware of the *look* of our hands on the handlebars, our feet on the pedals, the angle of the front wheel to the frame, the angle of the whole machine to the ground; these early visual images of the novice have been replaced by the awareness of movement sensations to do with pressing downwards, lateral adjustments and equilibrium, rhythmic action and speed; and visual images now are concerned with the relationship of body-and-machine together to the world around. But body-and-machine only remain as one unit as long as kinaesthetic awareness keeps them so. Any unusual demand upon the body-and-machine unit – whether foreseen, like a rise in the ground or an obstacle to avoid; or unforeseen, like a slipping chain – must be met and adjusted to kinaesthetically in order to maintain the overall continuity of movement.

For most of us, kinaesthetic sensations are recalled from memory by means of *visual images associated with movement;* it is easier to recall a *picture* of oneself swerving to avoid a dog – the look of the dog so close, the angle of the bicycle to the ground, the foot extended for momentary support, and the whole episode made continuous by thought – and then an 'echo' of the actual sensation of shock, swerve, unbalance, support, and recovery; it is almost impossible to recall a similar sensation entirely dissociated from visual relationships. We 'see' the event as a series of flashbacks, and the pictures are accompanied by the corresponding series of bodily sensations, in 'light relief' as it were. One particular sensation is powerfully re-lived by some people – the inner lurch which is associated with unprotected heights, uncomfortably recalled by photographs taken from the edge of a high cliff, or close-ups of steeple-jacks on high chimneys and steelworkers at the top of a pylon. For some, the experience of riding on a swing can be recalled by means of kinaesthetic imagery alone; but most of us have visual images of changing spatial relationships in the 'high-low-nearer-further' appearance of the world around; associated with this is the imprint of the bodily sensations of 'being swung' or 'causing to swing'.

This brings us to a consideration of active and passive roles in movement experiences, and the kind of imagery which accompanies them. In the case of 'being swung', the body quickly adjusts to the experience by means of the predictable rhythm, flow, and pathway of the movement; and for most of us this is a pleasing experience in which we can indulge ourselves – a positive attitude to our passive role. Any visual imagery arising is incidental, and a greater degree of awareness attaches to the kinaesthetic sensations. 'Causing oneself to swing' requires firm, direct, sustained action, which, in turn, needs a period of recovery; both are present in the action of swinging, where the greatest intensity of effort occurs part way along the forward pathway of the swing, followed by a phase of relative ease. But the main action in swinging oneself demands an attitude of 'fighting' weight and space, rather than indulgence in either, in order to achieve the desired result, and there is no doubt about the active role of the swinger. Here again, we are aware of kinaesthetic sensations, but we are also concerned with spatial relationships – how high can we push the swing (measured by relationship to the ground) before we can relax and enjoy the momentum we have created? Spatial relationships presuppose visual awareness, and we must deduce from this that any movements which alter the relationship of the mover to the world around him – running (from A to B), jumping (away from the floor), turning (from one side to another, and all the way round), signalling (arms to body), diving (piercing through air and water), stretching (taking up more space), curling (taking up less space), wriggling or twisting (around and through obstacles) – are also accompanied by visual imagery which is never entirely replaced or lost.

One particular experience needs special mention – that of falling. Certainly it alters the relationship of the mover to his surroundings, but insofar as he does not intend to fall, the experience finds him in a passive role, and therefore, overwhelmingly aware of sensation. However, (and unlike 'being swung'), he cannot indulge in this passive role, and immediately acts to save himself. But these actions are predominantly reflex, of the kind we have seen occurring in the young baby long before there is evidence of visual imagery. It would seem that falling is only tolerable if we are able to remain upright in the process (as judged by the sensitive balance mechanisms of the inner ear) or prepare ourselves for a particular landing by means of associated visual perception. If the fall is sudden and unexpected, and throws us out of the vertical, and if we are unable to orientate ourselves by means of visual perception the whole experience is entirely unpleasant, whether or not it results in injury. And it leaves us with a powerfully-imprinted sensation, readily recalled.

If we now consider the young child who has mastered walking, running, jumping, turning, throwing a ball, climbing a staircase, and hanging from a bar, we often find him practising these skills for no other reason than the pleasure he takes in their performance – 'playing', in fact; whereas his efforts to walk as fast as his father, to run away from a barking dog, to jump across a ditch, or to climb a tree for the first time require him to use these skills to meet a further challenge in his environment – to accommodate himself and his abilities to the expanding and demanding world around him – 'working', we might say. But climbing trees, jumping ditches, running away from the catcher in the playground game of 'Tag', may also be practised as play when they are not being used for the purposes of survival, since it is not in the nature of most young children (or young animals) to let such activities fall into disuse through lack of immediate need.

Piaget (1951) writes:

Play begins then with the first dissociation between assimilation and accommodation. After learning to grasp, swing, throw, etc., which involve both an effort of accommodation to new situations, and an effort of repetition, reproduction, and generalisation, which are the elements of assimilation, the child sooner or later (often even during the learning period) grasps for the pleasure of grasping, swings for the sake of swinging, etc. In a word, he repeats his behaviour not in any further effort to learn or to investigate, but for the mere joy of mastering it and of showing off to himself his own power of subduing reality.

We might consider that it is during any period of assimilation that kinaesthetic awareness develops to the point where it provides motivation for further practice because 'it feels good'. But if we wish to exploit this new consciousness in the child, we must make use of visual images, since language alone has no references. The young child cannot respond to suggestions like 'Grow tall' unless he has an image of something tall; so 'Grow tall like daddy' or perhaps 'Grow tall like the tree in the garden' gives him the necessary visual model to copy, and he discovers the anticipatory executional body-gesture of 'rising', together with its associated kinaesthetic imagery. He also acquires an elementary concept of growth. It may need reinforcing at first with the visual model of another person 'growing' in front of him, or it may not; the child may be content merely to stretch his arms above his head, but this is usually followed by a stretch throughout the body and an attempt to balance on the toes, for extra height. It is but a short step to the idea of starting close to the ground in order to obtain the maximum distance for the experience of 'growing'; and, once understood by the body, rising or growing upwards can be recalled kinaesthetically – but it began *in imitation of a visual model*, present or recalled.

Another source of kinaesthetic imagery arises when the

young child is scribbling for pleasure. Again, this is a 'play' situation, when the newly-acquired skill of marking with pencil or brush, can be practised, assimilated, made part of the child's sensory-motor equipment and enjoyed for its own sake before becoming a technique in the service of a further need. We can observe variation in the quality of his scribbles – some heavy and dark, some light and delicate, some jerky and uneven, some smooth and flowing – which indicates more than an erratic control of his pencil and brush; it shows an awareness of HOW to make marks as well as what shapes they can be and where to put them in the space. If we then draw attention to this aspect of scribbling – 'That is a strong and jerky pattern you are making. . .' or 'Here is a light and carefree pattern. . .' whilst the scribbling activity is in progress, the kinaesthetic awareness will be linked with a series of visual percepts, and with language. The language link is crucial if we wish to objectify movement qualities in the child and help him to use them consciously.

How else may the child arrive at an awareness of movement qualities – for instance 'slowly'? We have seen how a visual model may be used, to help him to 'grow upwards'; and this can be modified into 'suddenly growing upwards' because he can perceive the difference between sudden movements made by the growing model, and a prolonged movement, although he will find the latter more difficult to imitate; nevertheless, he will become aware of two relatively contrasting experiences. It is not at all easy for him to distinguish between heavy and light movements as they are performed by someone else, without the reinforcement of tactile experience; this may be provided by another person touching him lightly, and then moving lightly about the room; or by recalling his (recent) memory-image of a drifting snowflake which perhaps settled on his hand; or a feather, or a thistle-seed in flight. Eventually, his effort to move 'lightly' becomes patterned in the body, and requires no other model than itself, and moving 'heavily' is the contrasting experience.

Once the kinaesthetic awareness of movement qualities is established, the necessity for visual images decreases; and

Fig. 10. Firm and light, sudden and slow patterns painted by a girl aged five immediately after dance lessons.

moving lightly, heavily, suddenly, slowly, as one piece (directly), as many parts (flexibly), freely, or in a withholding kind of way, may be recalled entirely by means of kinaesthetic imagery; and may be experienced and observed as an aspect of body mastery and as a means of expression.

Finally, we should consider the possibility of perceptual concepts arising in the experience of movement – the kinaesthetic equivalent of Arnheim's (1966) 'roundness' in visual perception. In explaining his use of the term 'perceptual concepts' Arnheim writes:

> . . . we have to distinguish between the perceptual concept 'weight' which refers to the kinaesthetic experience of heaviness, and the intellectual concept 'weight', defined as the force with which the earth attracts an object. Both equally fulfil the requirements of concepts by being general qualities applicable to specific cases.

We must suppose that where imitation is involved *before* kinaesthetic awareness of a particular movement seems to exist, as in 'Grow tall like a tree', the perceptual concept (visually-established) of 'upness' or verticality applies. The eye imitates the 'up-and-up' appearance of the tree to form a mental image which is then imitated in a whole-body gesture (usually rapid) – thus producing the kinaesthetic image of 'rising'. Or, the mental image is imitated in arm-gestures which, by means of appropriate spatial organisation (hand to large paper fixed to the wall) and tools (pencil or brush), give the graphic image of a tall tree.

But in cases of incidental movement discoveries in which self-imitation *follows* the developing kinaesthetic awareness during a period of practice, play, assimilation – as in curling up tightly for comfort, stretching out on the floor, twisting and wriggling in a chair, moving from one place to another, jumping, turning, and keeping very still – other non-visual concepts may be formed. These could be concepts of 'doing' and 'not doing' – activity and stillness; and, later, of 'how I do' – the manner of doing – as in moving quickly, heavily, carefully. Other considerations of 'where' (upwards, forwards, along a straight line), and 'what part of me' (finger and thumb,

Fig. 11. Firm and light, sudden and slow patterns painted by a girl aged seven immediately after dance lessons.

hand, feet) involve visual perception, and take us beyond kinaesthetic experience alone.

And thus it would seem that only the most rudimentary dance activity could develop at this level, without the intervention of a teacher, since the perceptual concepts given to the child in the medium of kinaesthetic awareness limit him to patterns of movement and stillness, with heavy and lighter, quick and slower variations only – the nature of rhythm itself, and the basis of all dance forms. To develop beyond this, he must make use of visual perception; he must observe both himself (as much as he can see) and others around him in order to discover the perceptual concepts which will give the visual patterns to his dance – 'roundness' for a circle, 'directedness' for a line, and so on.

Arnheim (1956) writes at some length on 'the primordial circle', as do Sachs (1938), and Langer (1953); most of us are familiar with the idea of power, exclusiveness, magic and ritual invested in the circle of dancers; but it is interesting to take a further step backwards in the circle concept, by way of the young child's developing perception, to the dawn of mankind:

> ... intended roundness does not exist before other shapes, such as straightness or angularity, are available. At the stage of the circle, shape is not yet differentiated at all. The circle does not stand for roundness, but only for the more general quality of 'thingness' – that is, for the compactness of a solid object which is distinguished from the nondescript ground... (the child skipping his circle? the tribe gathering itself into a roughly circular shape?)... We are dealing here with what I shall call the law of differentiation. According to this law, a perceptual feature will be rendered in the simplest possible way as long as it is not yet differentiated. The circle is the simplest possible shape available in the pictorial medium. Until shape becomes differentiated, the circle does not stand for roundness, but for any shape at all and none in particular.

So, kinaesthetic awareness and its resulting imagery will provide an individual dance-like experience – at this stage, rhythmically-stressed and non-social. Visual perception and imagery will enable it to be moved into the arena as a social event, giving it solidity and distinction against its background, and shape and relatedness in its further development.

Awareness, Feeling and Perception

Two sources of imagery have thus been inferred – the two which have a direct bearing upon movement and drawing activities. We have seen how visual perception gives rise to the figurative image which can be imitated, by means of gesture, to give a graphic image on paper; and we have also seen how kinaesthetic imagery – the 'imprint' of bodily sensations associated with particular movements – may be used consciously in descriptive activities, such as 'moving heavily' or 'growing tall like a tree'. But we have also noted that kinaesthetic awareness often develops in association with other forms of perception.

The kinds of activity which stimulate movement awareness and, with it, the possibility of kinaesthetic imagery which may be recalled, could be summarised in the following way:

First, those in which a specific physiological cause brings about a movement, or movements, difficult to stop or control – as in yawning, stretching after cramped sitting, laughing or crying in shock; and those where visual perception is temporarily suspended because a physical or mechanical force acts upon us rapidly or unexpectedly – as in falling, or riding on a fast roundabout; in such situations we are in a relatively *passive* role, either at the mercy of our own bodily state, or deprived of our normal vision.

Second, where visual, aural, or tactile stimuli provide

motivation for the imitation of an action; examples of visual stimulation are throwing a ball repeatedly, scribbling purposefully, 'being a snowflake'; examples of aural stimulation are shaking a rattle repeatedly, clapping and stamping, sibilant and percussive mouth sounds; and of tactile stimulation – stroking fur, squeezing soft soap, snuggling down in bed. All these activities bring their own rewards through associated sensations, but in order to repeat them the child must also repeat (without an action model) the actions of throwing, or hissing, or stroking – which means that he must become aware of what Piaget and Inhelder (1970) call 'the anticipatory executional gesture' – ('gesture' here being extended to include the motor activity which is necessary to produce mouth-sounds, or the whole-body activity involved in 'snuggling'). It is interesting to note that the kinaesthetic awareness here belongs, in the main, to a gesturing limb or other body part rather than to the whole body.

Third, where kinaesthetic awareness is itself emphasised in order to bring about motor coordination as a first and vital stage in mastering a skill (usually involving a teacher) – as in learning to ride and control a bicycle in such a way that the eyes and mind are free to concentrate on traffic hazards; and in developing fluent speech and handwriting so that ideas may be communicated speedily; or in mastering gymnastic techniques on bars, beams, and boxes in order to become a secure and aesthetically-acceptable performer in demonstrations and competitions. The difference between this group and the second group is really one of degree, since both consist of self-motivated activites in which kinaesthetic awareness assists in the development of utilitarian movements – that is, movements which are serving a further purpose in the adaptation of the organism to the environment – as opposed to movements which express a present state of being; but in the second group, the rewards of the actions are sensory rewards – visual, aural, or tactile – whereas the rewards in the third group are psychological and/or social.

And fourth, when the body itself is used as an intentionally expressive entity, in order that needs, emotions, moods, and ideas should be communicated – as in social communication, mime, and dance. This fourth group clearly differs from the first group by *intention*; here, kinaesthetic awareness is the primary source from which to draw the right feeling for the right movement – an intentional act of selection on the part of the moving person, as opposed to an incidental feeling arising in a passive situation.

Visual perception is a vital 'receiver' and there can be no question of its major function in enabling the child to come to terms with his immediate environment, to discover his active relationship to it, to differentiate objects at increasing distances from himself, and thus create a sense of recognition and order – in short, to adapt to his slowly expanding world; and all drawing activities which attempt to 'capture' external objects, by way of mental imagery, and return them to the external world as graphic images, could be said to reinforce this process. What major function does kinaesthetic awareness have?

Generally-speaking, kinaesthetic awareness arises through a sense of well-being, of pleasure in the act of moving, of harmony through muscular coordination, of satisfaction in the deep breathing before sleep; or it may arise in challenging the body beyond its usual performance, so that if we choose to climb a snow-covered mountain or swim across a lake or practise free-fall techniques in parachute jumping we shall be acutely aware of the whole process of moving. And in such situations we are indeed 'coming to terms with' the world; as is the young child on the climbing frame, or sliding across frozen puddles, or riding a new bicycle. But most of us, by the time we are adults, have learnt to adapt to the world around us with the minimum of bodily effort and physical challenge, and are aware only of the extreme sensations of painful movement, or pleasure in the gradual cessation of activity as we relax into sleep; whereas visual perception remains an active receiver throughout life.

Pleasure in the gradual cessation of activity, or rest itself, are not desirable states of being for indefinite periods and certainly not as a way of life – no matter how appropriate the idea may seem at times of physical exhaustion or illness. The human body is a physical organism 'programmed' for activity, and rest is an incidental 'pause' which allows for recovery. The fine tuning of the organism has its key in the kinaesthetic awareness which makes possible a highly-sensitive reading at all times; and this is particularly valuable when unusual demands are being made upon the body – either in terms of intense or prolonged physical activity (as in athletics, for instance) or in terms of the quality of physical activity (as in dance); such awareness may lead to the desire to repeat activities (thus prolonging the 'good feeling'), or to the attempt to record the good feeling in the form of images which may be recalled at some future time. The actual nature of these images may be more complex than simply recalling a feeling would suggest; in comparative stillness, one may imagine the feeling of falling, or turning, or stretching, or jumping, and such imagery is usually accompanied by some faint muscular trace of those movements; this 'movement memory' is a necessary basis to the dancer's skill, just as word memory is to the actor's skill. But movement memory cannot concern itself solely with the kind and quality of a particular activity, or sequence of activities; it must also picture the relationship to the space around – 'stretching' . . . (to the ceiling or the sides?) . . . 'jumping' . . . (upwards or forwards?) . . . 'turning' . . . (all the way round?) . . . 'falling' . . . (to collapse on the ground?). So the recalled images are a kinaesthetic/visual mixture where-ever the art of movement is being practised; whereas the young child who 'prolongs the good feeling' by indulging in dance-like activities, whilst most certainly being kinaesthetically-aware, has not, as yet, begun to develop the image mixture which is the basis of movement as an art form.

Prolonging the good feeling is evidence of some degree of mastery over his body which, Piaget (1951) tells us, he practises for its own sake; there is also evidence that such activity (usually rhythmical in character) may be the young child's way of off-setting his discomfort as a result of some previously repressive situation, or of counter-balancing a way of life which tends to be physically inhibiting. Laban (1963) writes:

In the early stages of life all movements involve a large number of joints to such a degree that bodily stirrings are never confined to one joint alone. The total stir of the whole being is illustrated by the combination of kicking and making noises, which may have a parallel in the combination of song and dance in primitive folk-lore. It is obvious that when only one joint is moved, a repression of the rest of the bodily stir takes place. This repression has an inhibitive character which is felt as a discomfort as long as the urge to move is as intensive as it is with any normal child. The natural outlet for this inner tension is dancing, and this is apparently one of the causes of the urge to dance awakening in children at an age when the controlled use of a restricted number of joints has become habitual.

Whatever the motivation for dance and dance-like activities, this particular function of kinaesthetic awareness belongs only to the body itself, and cannot be used directly in relating to the environment. But if we, as sensitive observers, stand back from the movement activities of others and attempt to understand the *cause or intention* of what we see, we become aware of the impulsive and spontaneous character of young children's activities – (the sheer joy in the running, jumping, spinning, rolling, laughing activities of children suddenly free in an urban park; the anger and frustration in the stamping, hitting, screaming tantrum) – compared with the more controlled, descriptive character of later activities – (the exchange of ideas in the symbolic gestures which are practically uni-versal – inviting, rejecting, pleading, with-holding, embrac-ing, aspiring, submitting). And we understand not only some-thing of the feelings expressed in those movements because we are able to associate what we see with what we ourselves have felt (by means of visual/kinaesthetic recall), but also the value of educating such an ability in others in the cause of social relationships.

It is necessary, at this point, to look more closely at what we mean by 'feelings'. The word 'feeling' is used in a general way to stand for a private and personal capacity which we all have – something in us which responds to people and events in a peculiarly human way so that we 'warm' towards them, recoil from them (or are possibly unmoved by them – having, it seems, no feelings in the matter at all). We may also feel 'ill', 'cold', 'tired' – so that our use of the word has also a physical and observable aspect – since shivering, sickness, and exhaustion *are* our feeling, rather than *symptoms* of it – (they are more correctly, symptoms of the specific causes which led to the feelings). Clearly, feeling is *not* perception, since perception is specific to one of the five senses – visual, aural, tactile, olfactory, gustatory – though feeling may be used rather loosely to mean 'touch' (as in 'feeling the surface of the wallpaper'). And feeling is not thought, which is entirely mental in character.

In our general use of the word, the common element is the *physical character* inherent in 'feeling' – for instance, 'recoiling' is an action, even if it is withheld for the sake of social custom; 'coldness' is a physical state which may be recognised by the shivering movements or by the surface response of the body; 'sinking' and 'rising' are physical experiences directly related to gravitational force, which describe the physical character of our responses to particular events – 'a sinking feeling' before an examination, and the 'uplift' of an unexpectedly good result.

But in any discussion of the relationships between kinaesthetic awareness and the emotions (which would be relevant to our understanding, through observation and kinaesthetic / visual association and recall, of other people's movements) the meaning of the word 'feeling' must be specific, since it is used in association with both experiences, and often blurs the distinction between them.

'Feeling', as used in the present text, applies to the psycho-somatic character of any awareness of bodily tensions, whether voluntary or involuntary in origin. This covers the spontaneous activities of children which are then repeated – imitated – 'to prolong the good feeling'; the adaptation of the body to physical and mechanical forces – falling, being swung, staying on a fast roundabout, floating at the sea's surface; the surge of adrenalin in sudden fear (and readiness for fight or flight) and its accompanying muscular tensions; and all this again in anger; the enclosing nature of protective love; the spitting dismissal of hatred; the gentle flow of serenity; the aesthetic pleasure in the skilful performance of gymnastic activities, and in the rhythm, shape, and flow of dance of any kind; in fact, in any sphere of movement, however scaled-down, which is more than a purely functional motor skill for utilitarian purposes.

The dictionary definition of 'emotion' is 'agitation of mind, feeling; excited mental state'; this has certain shortcomings in the present context because it fails to indicate that emotion is the *effect* of a *cause*, rather than a fluctuating state. We could also define emotion as 'a spontaneous feeling response to a particular object or event'; this allows for the adjustment of bodily tensions – that is, *movement* – as the root of the word suggests; and it also points to a *cause*. If this is an acceptable definition, we must ask whether there is anything in that 'feeling response' which cannot be captured by means of kinaesthetic awareness, and used in a descriptive / artistic way by the actor-dancer, or as a means of understanding people in non-verbal communication? Returning to the children in the park, we observed impulsive, upward (jumping), onward-going (running, rolling, spinning) movements, accompanied by laughter (which has similar characteristics). What we see recalls our own experience of such movements, and even the faintest kinaesthetic 'trace' is enough to tell us that the children are joyful; we should recognise this at a much greater distance, with no sound and no facial expressions to reinforce it. Similarly, we might infer sadness, or anger, by means of movement observation.

Most of us are unaware of how much we 'read' people by their movements until we find ourselves trying to visualise the person at the other end of a telephone conversation; in a more usual face-to-face situation we think that we are concentrating upon what is being said, but we note the recurring shift of weight from which we infer physical or psychological unease, the eye-to-eye confrontation which reinforces the credibility of even the most outrageous statement, the rotating foot which may mean loss of concentration or a degree of impatience. A group of people engaged in conversation in total darkness will struggle to overcome the handicap of being unable to watch each speaker, by listening acutely for any nuance of voice which will indicate unseen attitudes. The desire to see the speaker only fades during an exchange of intellectual abstractions – when, indeed, a view of the speaker may prove an obstacle to logical thought!

All this serves to underline the fact that kinaesthetic awareness, vital as it is to its 'owner', can only contribute indirectly to communication; at the very least, an observer (a would-be receiver of communication) must use his visual faculties to 'read' the movements of another; and a signaller / actor / dancer (an intentional communicator) must use both kinaesthetic and visual imagery in order to convey the meaning of his movements. Arnheim (1956) reminds us of Michotte's point that:

> ... our dynamic body image has poorly-defined limits. It is a 'kinaesthetic amoeba'; it has no contour. Michotte explains that this is true because the body is the one and only content of the kinaesthetic field. There is nothing beyond and around it, no 'ground' from which it could detach itself as the figure. Thus we can judge the size and strength of our motions in relation to each other, but we have little concept of their impact in the surrounding visual field.

A moving person who wishes to communicate by means of his movements must consider their visual projection; and in order to receive his communication, an observer must use visual perception.

In this respect, dance and art share the medium of space, in which they are perceived by others as visual images. But here the similarity of the realised forms (the complete dance or painting) ends. Every instant of the dance requires a new act of visual perception; whereas the painting can be given in its entirety at any moment of perception, and subsequent acts of perception, though seeing it differently, will always see the whole in any one instant.

Not all dance is performed to communicate to an observer or audience (though paintings are always presented for visual perception), and in such cases, the dancers care rather less for its appearance, and rather more for its feel – the feel of the rhythmical patterns and the flow of movement, which belong entirely to the kinaesthetic experience (unlike the spatial patterns and considerations of role-relationships, which belong to the visual experience). Such dance is 'physiognomic' in character, rather than 'descriptive' (Arnheim 1956) – spontaneously reflecting the mood of the moment, rather than deliberately shaping the gestures to represent perceptual qualities. In brief, this kind of dance is very far from visual art.

Moving and looking are first differentiated in the baby when he learns to recognise (apprehend) objects by their appearance alone – their 'thingness' which detaches them from the general surroundings – without needing also to touch and hug them; that is, when he has visual awareness without the necessity of the accompanying tactile-kinaesthetic awareness. From this time, the two abilities are used increasingly for two different purposes; and although some children seem to retain the influence of the kinaesthetic sense in their visual world indefinitely, most seem relatively unaware of their immediate movement and touch sensations as they look at objects-to-draw, or recall objects from memory or imagination. But increasing skill in the drawing medium develops on an underlying kinaesthetic basis which gradually influences *how* the child sees the object-to-draw, and has to do with the feel of the pencil on the paper rather than with the feel of the object itself.

The very first drawing activity is accompanied by tactile-kinaesthetic awareness, so that the young child is conscious of the touch-and-movement involved, whether his gestures are entirely spontaneous or in imitation of someone else; but the 'thing drawn', whether a simple mark, or later a representation of MAN, soon becomes more important to the child than the 'act of drawing'. The 'thing drawn' may be a special scribble, a

71

representation of an inner state (earache, for instance), or the result of conscious control of the pencil or brush – 'suddenly and lightly' or 'twisting heavily'; or it may be (and most often is) a representation of some external object which has sufficient and significant outline shape in the child's visual percept for him to form a mental image or series of images which belong to the possibilities of the drawing medium.

The appearance of external objects to the child (the visual percept), and the 'drawing eye' (a particular act of perception) which receives that appearance in terms of 'what can be drawn' (the stimulus-in-terms-of-technique) are interdependent. So also are the 'act of drawing' (with its tactile-kinaesthetic awareness) which is an adaptation of basic gestures, and the 'drawing eye' interdependent. This, it seems, is where the artist begins to develop; it is a particular *manner of looking.*

The earliest self-motivated movement activities will be accompanied by kinaesthetic awareness, and may be associated with tactile, aural, or visual awareness also; the child will move for one of two main reasons – either to bring about an end result, such as moving a toy, or drawing a picture, or crossing a room, when the kinaesthetic awareness will be subordinate to visual factors; or he will move for the reward of *interest in moving,* as in rhythmically-stressed, dance-like activities, or in gymnastic / athletic-type activities such as running, jumping, rolling and swinging. The act of moving for interest is its own stimulus to continue moving in this way; when it is accompanied by sound it may be further stimulated as a result of aural perception; eventually, this partnership between moving-and-making-sounds (as in primitive song-and-dance) may develop into mainly vocal and instrumental activity (with the first instrument being the human body, clapping and stamping); this in turn may lead to the entirely aural experience of the *listener* to music – ultimately that kind of music in which all trace of organic rhythm with its weight-time-flow relationships has disappeared.

The act of moving rhythmically for its own sake may also lead on to an awareness of the visual shapes arising through movement as a result of kinaesthetic sensations; so that moving and looking become a partnership, in which the mover is aware that his movements express (externalise) his feelings in visual form; and this, too, becomes a self-rewarding experience – and the beginning of the development of the *expressively-intent* dancer.

The act of moving with expressive intention may draw an aesthetic or emotional response from an observer – depending upon the nature of the dance. Generally speaking, the aesthetic response arises in the presence of the expressive dancer whose feelings are embodied in forms which the observer receives visually as shapes and patterns of movement (trace forms arising from bending, stretching, and twisting activities of the limbs and body); and as qualities of movement also (impulsive, precise, controlled, impassioned – though extremes of these qualities, and abrupt changes between them, may introduce a dramatic character to the dance); such movement qualities arouse a kinaesthetic 'echo' in the observer, thus making his aesthetic response of a different order from that aroused by a purely visual art form; and this response has also an emotional component (if we understand 'emotion' to mean 'an excited mental state') even where the dancer has no intention to express or embody an emotion, as such, in the dance.

But a predominantly emotional response may arise in specific dance situations – either when the dance is spectacular and breathtaking; or when the dancers' *roles* become more important than the dance content. From expressively-intent dance, the emergence of contrasting movement characteristics, particularly between two dancers, ·or a dancer and a group, conveys tensions which are communicated to an observer without specific mime, or words. Watching this dramatic inter-play, and the corresponding facial gestures, he may 'identify' with one or other protagonist in the drama as it unfolds. Alternatively, he may feel an aesthetic response to the whole dance-drama as it moves towards impending doom or eternal delight. Where a solo performer re-creates an experience by 'acting-out' the sequence of events in terms of his own role in those events, the dramatic content may be more precisely conveyed by his use of mime – (particularly effective in humorous situations) – so that an observer receives, visually, a very detailed communication. But however the dramatic content is conveyed between performers, and from performers to audience, expressive movement is seen to have meaning beyond itself, and we see the development of the *actor-dancer*.

However, if the shapes and patterns of movement which so delighted the expressively-intent dancer become, instead, trace forms to delight the would-be artist, it is at this point that descriptive movements take on a perceptual quality which is seen in terms of paint-on-canvas in a predominantly linear form. There is no intention to suggest that 'linear' artists must first have been expressively-intent dancers! But there is strong evidence to support the idea that such descriptive movements, which are common to both, sustain an area of common interest, and a heightened awareness of the other's medium.

Not all painters begin from this linear stimulus; and we must suppose that, in general, the perception of any artist is not unlike that of the rest of us. But the particular inter-action of perceptual and emotional experience which motivates him to re-create the significant forms in pictures – the general form quality of 'treeness' which leapt to his eyes as he turned the corner in a country lane, or of 'towerness' in a modern, urban landscape – this interaction is the desired state of the would-be artist who must see these forms in terms of gesture and paint-on-canvas in order to realise them. In Arnheim's (1956) words:

> ... the conception of the form by which the conceived structure of the object can be represented with the properties of a given medium ... (this) more than anything else distinguishes the artist from the non-artist. Does the artist experience the world and life differently from the ordinary man? There is no good reason to think so. He must be deeply concerned with – and impressed by – these experiences. He must also have the wisdom of finding significance in individual occurrences by understanding them as symbols of universal truth ... the artist's privilege is to apprehend the nature and meaning of an experience in terms of a given medium and thus make it tangible.
>
> ... Why do some landscapes, anecdotes, or gestures 'ring the

74

bell'? Because they suggest, in some particular medium, significant form for a relevant truth. In search of such telling experiences, the artist will look around him with the eyes of the painter, the sculptor, the dancer, or the poet, responding to what fits his form. . .

And finally –

The medium itself is a powerful source of inspiration. It often suggests form elements that turn out to be usable for the expression of experience.

For artist and dancer, this is equally true.

Dance and Art

Dance and the visual arts begin when moving and looking are accompanied by a particular kind of awareness which lifts these normally utilitarian activities onto another level, and orders the immediate or recalled experiences into finite 'statements' which are thus separated from the on-going experiences of everyday life. Such 'statements' reflect their origins, and show awareness of both moving and looking in varying proportions, according to the gestural skill and the vision of the dancer and the artist. As a child, the dancer moved for the pleasure of moving, liked his partial view of himself in movement (or of others moving) and continued the experience; thereafter, *moving and looking became a continuous partnership*, but with the kinaesthetic factor being the fundamental element – without which the dancer might have become a painter or a sculptor, perhaps. As a child, the artist moved for the pleasure of moving, liked the marks which movement left behind, and continued marking with whatever tools came to hand; thus *moving* – the painting /chiselling/moulding gesture – *is always in the service of looking,* and yet modifies what the artist sees.

Dance as we know it today has three main aspects – rhythmical, expressive, and dramatic. Rhythm is present in all dance forms, and the dancer is always aware of the rhythmic patterns, whether 'free' or metrical. To the observer, all dance is also expressive – of physical ability, purpose, country, class, and mood, for instance – though the waltzing couples in the ballroom may only be aware of the rhythm, and of each other. But all dance has some particular character to both dancer and observer as a result of its *stressed* aspect, so that rhythm, expression, or drama is the predominant feature.

Rhythmically-stressed dance is first an individual response to a physiological urge, which later becomes a group response to a social urge as the rhythm becomes both visible and audible, and provides a unifying factor; and it is most clearly felt in the body-centre, and in weight-changes from foot to foot.

Expressively-intent dance is concerned with the quality and shaping of gestural movements particularly – (though these may be extended to include 'bodily gestures') – which occur in conjunction with certain physical sensations; thus the dancer might perform a rising, opening movement of the whole body and the arms, repeated three times with increasing strength of impulse and size of gesture. Or he may perform movement phrases which are recalled in association with feeling-states, such as the downward stress of sadness, relieved only by the slight lift on the indrawn breath; or the upward stress of gaiety, renewed by repeated impulses. There are movements which seem to portray abstract ideas, like flight or growth; and those which occur in response to visual stimuli, like curves and angles; or aural stimuli, like machine sounds, or music.

Dramatic dance is concerned with tension and conflict in relationships between individuals, and groups, and in the inevitability of events stemming from those conflicts.

Expressively-intent dance in its early stages is, for the solo dancer / choreographer, self-gratifying and autonomous – the centre of a world in which 'I move as I feel' is the major criterion of dance-design; and where personal and characteristic movement patterns may be indulged in, practised, assimilated, in a form of artistic play. The further challenge to create new and different dances may then lead the dancer to observe the world around him, and incorporate into his movement repertory other patterns which characterise other moods and express other ideas. Yet there will still be something uniquely personal in his presentation of dance, so that an audience may watch in much the same way as it might look at a painting – seeing the expression or embodiment of a very personal form of perception – the dancer's or the artist's own.

Dance has, by this stage, moved away from the possibility of active participation by all in the shared rhythmical structure (as in various forms of social dance); it has become an art form for the individual dancer, and it has left the arena and entered the theatre. Within the framework of a particular dance technique, many dancers may be trained to perform movements expressive of the uniquely personal characteristics of their choreographer – himself similarly trained – or he and they together may compose a dance whose style and content has its roots in their common training, but whose theme and structure is the choreographer's own. A particular achievement of classical ballet is the training which enables a corps de ballet to dance 'as one' within the medium of expressive gesture, as in Fokine's 'Les Sylphides'. For such dancers, the necessity to adapt their skills to the requirements of the choreographer removes their dance experience from the realm of 'artistic play' into the realm of work; but for the choreographer some element of 'play' may be retained; the dancers and their skills are the raw material of his chosen medium, as are paint and canvas that of the artist; and both choreographer and artist may prolong the period of 'artistic play' in the practice and repetition of favourite techniques, motifs, and themes, until a fresh stimulus sets them on a new course of exploration and invention.

One such stimulus may arise through the close association of the arts, and is often seen as evidence of fundamental relationships between art forms. In the search for new stimuli or by way of active response to the appeal of a given art work – for instance, Isadora Duncan's dance in response to the Ninth Symphony of Beethoven; and Mussorgsky's music in response to Hartmann's design for the Great Gate of Kiev – the dancer / musician / artist may translate the stimulus into his own medium by means of intentional symbolism; his subjective response to the given art work may find embodiment in another art form, and there have shape and unity in its own right, standing apart from the stimulus. If it cannot stand apart – (and dance to music is a case in point) – this is not proof of integration, but (some musicians would say) of parasitism, since the original art work – the stimulus – is a complete statement without need of adjuncts. If, however, the two events – the composition of the music and of the dance – happen together, and are thus integral to the total music / dance composition, intentional symbolism of forms from one medium to another need not occur. Together, the music and the dance make a totality – an art work with unity – but apart, they are each incomplete, and neither can stand alone. The association between dance and music has for so long been accepted that the absence of music sometimes precludes dance, because a dancer feels no stimulus to move without it. Yet if dance is worthy of acceptance as a major art form, it must exist in its own right and not solely as a visual extension of sound. Such visualisation is a subjective process in which the dancer symbolises the ordered sounds in appropriate movements. But the 'ordering' was first achieved by the composer in the medium of sound, and was a complete statement – a unity – in that medium. The sustained stimulus of sound may prevent the dance from achieving a unity in its own terms, and thus it cannot exist satisfactorily without the music.

Similar examples occur between visual art and dance, in the use of elaborate masks to portray, for instance, strange creatures of supernatural powers; these masks stimulate appropriate movement qualities in which the dancer intentionally symbolises the character implied by the mask. Without the mask, the dance loses much of its import. But without the movement, the mask remains a complete statement in its own medium. If, however, the dancer moves with trailing, swirling, enveloping drapes which take on new qualities in movement and create extended trace forms in the space around, the dance and the kinetic art form are together creating a unity, and either without the other is pointless movement or nondescript fabric.

If an artist sets out to symbolise movement in his canvases by devices to suggest speed or gravitational pull or explosions, this in no way makes him a kinaesthetic artist, nor is his work an example of integration. But the action painter who is as much aware of the gestural qualities behind the marks as he is of the marks themselves must work with a succession of images resulting from a constant 'dialogue' between visual perception and kinaesthetic recall – one possible approach to re-integration of these two activities.

Rhythmically-stressed dance has its true basis in the organic rhythms of the body. This is perhaps most clearly shown in primitive dance, but the pattern of development echoes that of the movement development of the baby and the young child – thrusts outward from the centre with the gesturing limbs, pushing-away and gathering-in, stamping and clapping, jumping and turning, accompanied by all the vocal sounds that occur naturally with such strong efforts. The organic rhythm of breathing will govern the frequency of jumps, for instance, or of any strong effort requiring total bodily participation. Heightened awareness of the heart-beat or pulse rate – which occurs particularly after exertion or at times of great excitement – gives a basic time-unit for stamping and clapping, with the possibility of stressed beats which link with breathing and create 'measures'. Once the acoustic background has been revealed in sound, it becomes available to others around and serves as a unifying force so that all may share in the common rhythm. We know how infectious these kinds of sounds can be – particularly if they grow out of an organic basis which is common to everyone. Add to this an urge to celebrate – freedom after confinement, victory after battle, togetherness after separation, security after fear – and you have cause for dance; and the power of dance may be used to ward off unknown terrors, to promote fertility in the tribe, to ensure a major kill in the hunt, a victory over trespassers, sun and rain for the crops.

With such a sense of involvement, there arises also the beginnings of social organisation – a sense of corporate responsibility, of corporate power; and the emergence of certain individuals with, perhaps, more energy, greater stamina, better ideas than others, who become dance leaders, shamans, magicians, and eventually intermediaries (priest-kings) who hold the tribe at one remove from the unknown. In primitive societies there is no doubt about the major function of dance – physiological, social, religious – from its earliest rhythmically-stressed movements to the stylised ritual gestures of the masked intermediaries. What have we now?

The true descendant of the early rhythmically-stressed dance is to be found in any arena large enough to contain all who come – folk dance on the village green, waltzes in the ballroom, the rock and beat of the disco. It is not found on any stage which presupposes an audience, nor in any religious ritual performed only by priest and acolyte. Nor is it found among groups of dedicated dancers within our educational institutions who work long and hard at technical mastery, the fine nuances of expression, and intellectual concepts of the body in space; theirs is a different goal, an art form. Rhythmically-stressed dance occurs in all kinds of societies; it is the dance of the people, 'lay' dance, participation – in spite of the constrictions imposed by the mastery of intricate steps and complex floor patterns. It flourishes in spite of changing cultural patterns, showing a cyclic development from the open (partnerless, 'free') forms of early societies, through increasingly closed forms of partner dances with restrained, precise movements, back to the open form of the discotheque. The decline of one form (say, jiving) coincides with the birth of another (twisting). All this suggests that it still fulfils its physiological and social functions, at least among the young; theoretically, it is open to all, and only diminishing energy, stamina, and social need lead to its decline.

This dance arises in the very act of living, and its movements transmit this life directly to the external world – they are unconcerned with self-expression, with symbolism, or with communication – simply with 'being'. At this level of moving in response to a physiological need, and practising these movements because they bring pleasure and satisfaction in the performance – (Piaget's 'assimilation') – I find a close parallel with the 'purposive pencillings' (Burt 1922) in the scribble stage of the young child. When some form of social

81

organisation begins to occur in dance through imitation of a dance leader – the 'accommodation' by the dancers to certain stressed movements, or particular floor patterns – the parallel is extended to include 'imitative pencillings'. When the dancer assumes the role of another person or creature in order to use the dance for some purpose beyond itself – for instance, animal movements in a hunting dance – the parallel may be further extended to include the young child's attempts to represent external objects in his drawings. We have now moved from kinaesthetic drawing activities to representations, and from rhythmically-stressed dance to dramatic dance.

Dramatic dance is, by definition, an integration of two art forms as we know them today – dance and drama. I use 'integration' advisedly here, rather than 'combination', for reasons which will emerge. Integration is evident in the use of the sequential or 'dialogue' form which, in speech or body-language or both, communicates powerful tensions, passions, and conflicts from one actor-dancer to another, or between an actor-dancer and the intangible or invisible powers of his imagined world – all of them moving onwards towards an inevitable end or destiny. Our reconstructions of dance in prehistory suggest that dance-drama may have been one of the earliest of the known art forms; the cave paintings of Paleolithic hunters show a masked man 'dancing' among the animals, and from Stone Age cultures in our own time, we infer that he is practising a 'magic' by imitating the head, and the movements of an animal, perhaps to bring success in the hunt; and the cave artists may have reinforced that magic by making a permanent record on the rock. Rock paintings of bushmen show similar relationships of an apparently dancing man to animals in his immediate world. It could be argued that the earliest cultures reflect the pre-differentiation stage of today's young child, and that the 'higher' art forms are the result of a long process of refinement; alternatively, such refinement may be seen as a major threat to any sense of the 'wholeness' of life through an awareness of the recurrent patterns in an individual's total experience. Wherever one might choose to stand in such an argument, the problem of reintegration remains for those who have concurred in the separation of the dance and the drama elements at any stage; and similarly, for those who separate dance from music, or music from dance; drama from visual representation; poetry from drama; poetry from music; and sculpture and architecture from each other. But for those whose experience of dance has always been within the dramatic mode – for magical, ritualistic, religious or theatrical purposes; and as part of a total expression of man's understanding of life, with masks, head-dresses, imitative or traditional costumes, symbolic props, and atmospheric lighting; speech, chanting, instrumentation – the problem of reintegrating elements which, in their experience, have never been separated within the whole is irrelevant because it is beyond perception.

But in the perceived problem of reintegrating dance with art, we have two stages of dance development to consider – the first and fundamental stage of kinaesthetic awareness, (which may produce a satisfying graphic record as a result of movement activities with suitable tools); and the second, 'artistic', stage of partial visual perception which leads to a new ordering of kinaesthetic awareness, to enhance *what is seen*. This second stage – the visual awareness of shape, direction, import and relationship – is the area in which dance and art may merge; either in the perception of basic patterns in the kinaesthetic 'scribbles' which stimulate imitation or further exploration (particularly, with young children, in a sensitive and sympathetic educational context); or in the perception of increased enhancement of the body-image for the dancer. Such enhancement of the body-image may increase the expressive character of the dance, by means of flowing drapes or rigidly-stylized costumes, for instance, or by means of colour and light; it may deepen characterisation or personification by means of masks, costumes, props, and décor. But enhancement of the body-image, above all, presupposes a concern with other people and their reactions; with attempts to control the powerful physical forces in the real world, whose nature is not fully-understood; with the need to reflect, in the theatre, the unceasing conflict of man against man, or man against nature;

and such a concern is the very essence of dramatic dance which communicates character, story, tension, passion and conflict arising from the strivings of the dancers-in-their-roles to accommodate themselves to the world-in-the-dance and achieve a stable equilibrium. A mask alone can portray power, inhumanity, evil, pathos, an archaic divinity, animism. Masks and dancers together can realise the import of the fixed visual image in a series of sequential images which give life and depth to the characters, and convey the events of their story.

Yet even here, when the mask-maker might himself put on the mask and compose the dance, or the dancer might evolve, mentally, the mask which belongs to his dance and then make it – even here, two distinct sets of images are involved; one set will 'see' the mask not only as a character, but in terms of its structure – clay, papier-mâché, wood or cloth – and its colours; and the final image will be the finished statement – the mask itself, complete in three spatial dimensions, whereas the other set will be externalised and shaped in a linear dimension of time, each one 'seeing' a momentary part of the whole dance but all of them evident in the finished statement, and all of them dependent upon the underlying kinaesthetic imagery which is at the recall of every dancer.

Since the purpose of this study is to look closely at movement and painting relationships particularly, and, from them, at dance and art, it is necessary to return to the kinaesthetic 'scribbles' which arise directly from a common source with dance-like activities, and to see what kind of art form – if any – might emerge.

Briefly summarising the development of the two activities, we have seen that drawing and painting activities often arise as a direct result of visual perception and the motivation to 'capture' the external image in concrete form; they are made possible by gestural movements (accompanied initially by kinaesthetic awareness) having their own trace forms and qualities which mould the drawing and painting techniques. But a particular kind of drawing activity, in which the trace forms are a record of movement pathways and move-ment qualities only, depends primarily upon kinaesthetic awareness; and only involves visual perception when there is an attempt to 'order' the resulting trace forms and qualities into a satisfactory visual composition – that is, to turn a satisfactory movement experience into a satisfactory picture.

Movement activities may arise for one of several reasons:- simply, the need to move rather than to be still; or in the expression of feeling-states (of pleasure, perhaps) or an emotion (possibly anger), when the movements are characteristic of such feelings; or from the desire to imitate an action, the results from which have previously been perceived visually, aurally, or by touch – and the performance of which action requires the associated kinaesthetic awareness and therefore the beginning of *kinaesthetic imagery;* or from the desire to communicate to others, when success must depend upon visual control and reception if speech is not in order.

Dance activity grows from the same sources, but kinaesthetic awareness alone is not sufficient; it must be accompanied by its own imagery – an ability to 'focus' the mind upon a particular bodily experience in order to recall it again at will; this gives the dance *organic form within its own medium,* rather than purely visual form arising from the imitation of visual images only – (at best, a series of rapid 'stills' connected by thought rather than by necessity). Yet visual perception is vital where there is any intention to communicate; the source of a dancer's imagery should be, primarily, kinaesthetic, until it is externalised in movement, when the visual forms and relationships make it available to others, and also enable the dancer to see, partially, with their eyes.

The source of an artist's imagery may be directly visual – the landscape, the still life, a particular face; or it may be imaginative – the result of a fusion of ideas and images; it may be intentionally symbolic, with light standing for wisdom and a closed door for the obtuseness of the world; or academic, with a picture 'emerging' from a structure suggested by the rules of classical composition; or the medium itself may supply the images, as in an exploration of colour values and light; it could be kinaesthetic in origin, when movement experiences and their graphic results are recalled. Many artists are aware of the influence of movement upon their techniques, but few set out to record movement itself in the graphic image; Jackson Pollock was one of the few.

Jackson Pollock

Jackson Pollock talked about the supremacy of the *act* of painting as in itself a source of magic, and Harold Rosenberg immediately coined the new phrase 'Action Painting'.

Pollock said little about his painting in public, but that little, together with the careful observations of people who had the opportunity of watching him work, gives a clear exposition of how this artist formed his work in his chosen medium:

I don't work from drawing or colour sketches. My painting is direct... The method of painting is a natural growth out of a need. I want to express my feelings rather than illustrate them. Technique is just a means of arriving at a statement. When I am painting, I have a general notion as to what I am about. I *can* control the flow of paint; there is no accident, just as there is no beginning and no end.

Robertson (1960) writes of his work:

The drawings and studies ... 1930-1934 ... embody in the simplest terms his essential characteristics as an artist. The first impression is of an almost incessant preoccupation with movement... The figures are static but they share in common a declamatory note, almost of rhetoric. A dynamic attitude emerges imposed over the basic subjects... There is less concern for the human body than for the marks made on the paper and the way in which the casing of contour lines and structural accents combine together to make new

87

abstract shapes that are independent of the complete figure. Even in these early studies Pollock is trying to get through and beyond the restrictions of physical reality and to capture and transmit a distillation of energy, drawn out of the flux of human experience and thrown back again into the flux of time.

His later work was never consciously representational, although there are traces of recognisable forms and symbols, often relating to those influences which helped to shape his development as an artist – the sand-paintings, the culture, and the mythology of the Navaho Indians; for them, the act of 'painting' – (predominantly linear markings made by spilling sand and coloured earth through their fingers onto the ground) – is a means of communication between themselves and their gods, and the marks must all be erased by sunset; such art is a part of living, as were the paintings on the walls of caves, the rock paintings of bushmen, the pavement graffiti of children; but increasingly, since the Renaissance, art has become a specialist occupation, presented within the boundaries of a picture-frame, and hung under special lighting in purpose-built galleries. This art has not the same function in life today as the power-invoking, possession-taking graphic activities of the prehistoric hunter; yet Pollock (1947-48) seems to have dealt with his canvases in a not dissimilar manner; he wrote:

> My painting does not come from the easel. I hardly ever stretch my canvas before painting. I prefer to tack the unstretched canvas to the hard wall or the floor. I need the resistance of a hard surface. On the floor I am more at ease. I feel nearer, more a part of the painting, since this way I can walk around it, work from the four sides and literally be in the painting. This is akin to the methods of the Indian sand-painters of the West. I continue to get further away from the usual painter's tools such as easel, palette, brushes, etc., I prefer sticks, trowels, knives and dripping fluid paint or a heavy impasto with sand, broken glass and other foreign matter added.

Goodnough (1951) writes of Pollock:

Fig. 12.   'Blue Poles' by Jackson Pollock. (Oil, duco and aluminium paint on canvas. Detail approx 25 x 38 cm from original 260 x 480 cm. *(Coll. Australian National Gallery).*

The paint, usually enamel, which he finds more pliable – is applied by dipping a small house-brush or stick or trowel into the can, and then, by rapid movements of the wrist, arm, and body, quickly allowing it to fall in weaving rhythms over the surface. The brush seldom touches the canvas, but is a means to let colour drip or run in stringy forms that allow for the complexity of design necessary to the artist.

Pollock did not describe in words how the scale of his paintings related solely to the sweep of the gestures whose trace-forms were the components of his art, perhaps supposing this to be self-evident. But Robertson (1960) is fully aware of this identification of gesture and mark:

> . . . the measure in space of the marks made in each picture and their duration in time across the surface exactly embody the duration of the gesture made by Pollock and the measure of his scale as a man acting as *deus ex machina*. This particular unity does not exist in other artists' work because the scale contained in their pictures and the painting gesture which determines the scale are both at the service of a formal idea or design, absolutely independent in its measurements, that lives as a separate entity outside and away from the physical boundaries of the canvas: the accomplishment of the idea does not depend upon the circumscribed physical limitations, in terms of gesture, of the artist.

'Blue Poles' (1953) is widely regarded as one of Pollock's most important works. Robertson (1960) sees much in it of significance, and describes it vividly in movement terms; particularly:

> The span of movement behind the gesture, the action involved in making the gesture, is caught, trapped, and held on the surface of the picture. The whiplash line, the solid projection in paint of the gesture, is thrown out into the flux of time and space and instantly recorded.

Between 1951 and 1952, Pollock abandoned the use of colour and confined himself to black and white. Italo Tomassoni (1968) describes this as a period when Pollock tried to give maximum concentration to the sign, painting only in black and white so that no energy or expressive violence should be wasted in the registration of colour, but everything should be condensed and intensified in a single, monochrome statement. He is concerned with Pollock's relationship to space and time:

> Pollock 'is' in space simply by being in contact with objects other than himself; first and foremost the canvas, the locus on which he realises an event by flinging himself upon it, occupying it physically and conferring upon it the specific character of an area of space during a certain period of time . . . space is a physical expression of the artist himself and is entirely within his control. . . If the traces that an artist leaves in time constitute his deeds, the traces that he leaves in space should correctly be called his signs. If Pollock had confined himself to deeds he would have been a dancer or an actor; his action painting represents the deed of a moment in time made tangible in the form of a sign. By becoming visible, it ruptures the bonds of time as a dimension, breaking off its passage by taking on the opaque and finite substance of paint.

Pollock explored many variations and combinations of the four fundamental trace-forms (as described by Laban, 1966), sometimes in black and white, more often in colour. But he did more than this; every gesture was more than a purely spatial action; each was intensified by the 'inner attitudes' (Laban 1960) which determine the strength, flow, and duration of the gesture, and the bodily focus behind it. If we wish to analyse the graphic signs which fill his canvases, we need not regard them as symbols of his subconscious mind, nor need we wait for the underlying theme to reach us by intuition; instead, we may apply the same technique of observation and analysis as we would to Pollock's gestural movements – had we been there at the time of the painting activity.

Movements have force; they have duration in time; they have direction and extension in space; and they have flux – the normal continuation of movement which may be interrupted intermittently or stopped altogether. Laban (1960) referred to these as the weight factor, the time factor, the space factor, and the flow factor; and as a result of his observations of movements in the playground, on the street, in the factory, and on the stage, we have a technique for analysis which can be applied in any situation of human movement where the *manner* of moving is of particular importance. These factors of weight, time, space and flow are measurable; but human movement has also a 'felt' inner aspect, subjective and psychosomatic, which 'colours' the movements of, say, an angry, or dreamy, or alert person in particular ways, so that the observer is aware of characteristic movement qualities which are both interesting in themselves and revealing of the mover – that is, they are *expressive*.

We both observe, and experience, the four motion factors in terms of the two elements which constitute the opposing poles of each factor and the degrees of change between them; thus we *observe* force (the weight factor) in terms of firmness, or of fine touch; and we *experience* it ourselves as a feeling of strength, or of delicacy. We observe the duration of a movement (the time factor) as sustainment, or as suddenness; we experience it as a feeling of lingering, or of momentariness. We observe direction and extension (the space factor) in terms of directness, or of flexibility; we experience it as a thread-like movement, or as pliancy and ubiquity. And we observe flux (the flow factor) as free and on-going, or as bound and tightly-controlled movement; whilst we experience it as a streaming-out, uninhibited feeling, or as a feeling of 'withholding'.

This aspect of human movement – the manner of moving – is concerned with the effort content; and the two opposing elements of each motion factor were named by Laban (1960) 'effort elements'. But not only do we observe and experience the extremes of these elements, but also all possible gradations between them; and whilst any particular movement may show (or be experienced as having) one element clearly outstanding, that element is part of a combination of effort elements – of two, or three, or even of four – each belonging to a different motion factor. From what we observe, and recollecting what we have experienced, we are able to infer something of the feeling in the movements of others, and thus something of their personalities (from their characteristic use of their effort capacity); or something of their emotional state (from associated effort-element combinations); or something – usually a great deal – of the character or mood they are portraying, as dancers, actors, or both.

When we look at human movement in this way, we may see that one element from each of two motion factors is particularly evident (though traces of other motion factors are normally present); for instance, a sudden, direct movement (having a positive attitude to both time and space) characterises an alert person; and a sustained, freely-flowing movement (having a positive attitude to time and flow) characterises an easy adaptability. Sometimes one element from each of three motion factors is clearly present, so that we may see a sustained, firm, direct movement (time, weight and space) in the basic effort action required to push a piano across a room; whereas a sustained, firm, extremely-controlled movement (time, weight and flow) with no clear attitude to space, characterises a person of strong emotion. When an element from all four motion factors is clearly present in movement, we are most probably watching a dancer, whose entire effort capacity, in whatever combinations he chooses, is at the service of expressive, dramatic and rhythmical needs, rather than utilitarian and workaday needs. And an artist with such an effort capacity at his command may, through arm gesture rather than full body gesture, extend his painting techniques until they fully reflect the potential of human movement.

In the works of Jackson Pollock we can see various combinations of effort elements made permanent in graphic form. The weight and time changes in the black and white painting called 'Number Thirty-two' produce a clearly rhythmical effect; the space-weight relationships in 'Blue Poles', with the delicate, meandering tracery of silver, yellow, and orange, balanced by the straight, powerful, pole-like structures, give an effect of stability; the space-time 'busyness' of the ink, pencil, and water-colour drawing suggests a concentrated awareness. The early drawings have a freely-flowing line, heightened by the draped figures of the subjects which seem on the verge of mobility.

This is, of course, an unverifiable reading of the permanent graphic record of his gestures and the feelings they may have expressed – rhythm, stability, concentrated awareness. But whether or not the reading is accurate, or significant, Pollock would have at his command a whole range of possibilities for expression. By recalling, as the dancer recalls, kinaesthetic imagery associated with violent movements, for instance – (since it is said that he was much preoccupied with the phenomenon of violence in our society) – he could create a canvas of 'violence' in which the only non-movement element would be that of colour; it would not be a specific act of violence pictured there, but rather an abstraction of all physical violence seen in terms of effort and gesture. By such an abstraction, according to Arnheim (1966), does the young child begin to perceive and give order to the world of his experience. Perhaps the artist also, by more sophisticated means, may order his experience and thus grasp something of the nature of violence.

Not all of Pollock's paintings belong to the 'Action' class entirely, and some show distinctive representational features even among the trace forms. This has led some observers to write in terms of the symbolic nature of his work, drawing upon the early cultural influences particularly as sources of totem-like objects in some of the paintings. It may be that Pollock was aware of the symbolic nature of some pictures, or of images in those pictures; but since the bulk of his later work clearly belongs in the 'Action' class, we may assume that he had found there a rich source of imagery which made possible a direct and uncomplicated statement in paint, with no intentional symbolism of reality, or of myth. Yet the use of the symbol in art generally, and in dance and the visual arts in particular, has sometimes led to the assumption that integration should not only be possible at any level, but that separation has never actually occurred. It would be helpful, finally, to look at the use of the term 'symbol', and where it may lead us in our thinking about Integrated Arts.

The Symbol

The artist's *manner of looking*, in which he sees a particular view or imagined view in terms of the executional gesture and paint-on-canvas is, in itself, a form of symbolism – each line, each mass, each colour stands for the relevant element in his visual percept. But such symbolism is not at the forefront of his conscious activity, because the stimulus-in-terms-of-technique is an act of perception, and not a lengthy debate; 'seeing in a particular way' is concerned with the practicalities of re-creating the image in paint on canvas, and not with understanding the philosophy underlying his activity.

The dancer's *interest in moving* could end there – as moving for pleasure; and there is no symbolism involved because, unlike the painter, there need be no transference of idea to medium – no 'this' standing for 'that' – but just a prolonged extension of the interesting feeling by means of rhythm and flow. Such dance-like activities do not, of themselves, make a dance. And it is in the selection and arrangement of movements towards a finite dance 'statement' that the dancer's instrument (his moving body) and the idea for the dance (the stimulus) can be parallelled with the technique-plus-stimulus of the painter – when each movement made by the dancer 'stands for' a particular movement element in the dance image. But, like the painter, the dancer is concerned with the practicalities of re-creating the dance image in its external medium, having seen, at each moment of perception, the stimulus-in-terms-of-technique. And he is not concerned with the awkward philosophy of himself as both instrument and as image – which is peculiar to the dancer-choreographer whose art centres, physically, upon himself. The painter's materials and technique allow him to re-create an image which then stands apart from its creator, as a painting to be contemplated; whereas the dancer's materials and technique (his body, and the movements of his body) will only allow for the re-creation of an image which cannot stand apart from its creator. If the choreographer uses other dancers as his materials, and their movements (under his direction) to give shape and form to his image, the parallel with the painter's processes is sustained, insofar as his material is external to himself, and 'inanimate' until he gives it life. But the 'life' given to paint on canvas is entirely that as designed by the artist – there is no intermediate stage of *interpretation* by his materials during the realisation of his image. Whereas the life given to the choreographer's material – (the dancers' responses to his design) – has always an interpretative stage, which the choreographer cannot entirely predict, and for which his dance design will make allowances. This interpretative stage arises in the personal and unique kinaesthetic experience of each individual dancer, and results in a distinctive way of moving which may even persist throughout years of training and 'grooming' towards a corps de ballet ideal. Beyond this again lies *the conscious interpretation of the role* given to the dancer in the dance. Paint on canvas has no equivalent 'life' which is beyond the prediction and control of the artist. But in both cases, the symbolism is already there, in the act of perception which marks the genesis of creative activity.

It is at this same level of 'genetic' symbolism that music most often enters the dance. For many dancers, the stimulus-in-terms-of-technique is not an image of *movement* events which are then symbolised by the dancer as dance elements, but an image of *music* elements which he symbolises in movement; the rise and fall of a melody, the dynamic qualities, the metrical rhythm, the climax and resolution – all these will give shape and character to the dance. For example, a dance to the 'Air' from Bach's Suite Number Three in D will take its form and qualities from that music, and will be lyrical in character. Other images may indeed interpose themselves – the dance may occur in a religious context which would suggest a particular 'role' for the dancer; the music may convey a mood which could be intensified by costume and lighting; but the dance image arises, first and foremost, as a result of the stimulus given to the dancer by his perception of an *already realised form* – the musical composition. And, as with the painter, the symbolic aspect of this activity rarely enters the dancer's consideration.

This 'genetic' symbolism, whilst supporting the case for the association of dance with music (though a one-way relationship in terms of dependency), in no way assists the cause of integrating dance with art. If a particular act of perception gives a painterly image, this is not only in terms of the executional gestures (which may be easily transferred to the medium of dance-like activities) but in terms of mass, texture, colour – all given for contemplation at one and the same time. Whereas the dancer's awareness which gives rise to the dance image consists of sequential movements in a dynamic event which has a future, a present, and a past, even as it is performed – and all this must be given in the dancer's vision of the dance.

There are symbols which are used with *intent* by some artists, and some dancers. The symbol in art is an iconographic symbol; these symbols appear as part of a painting and clearly have meaning in the total import of the work. In 'Problems of Art', Langer (1957) writes:

> Some artists work with a veritable riot of symbols; from the familiar halo of sacrosanct personages to the terrible figures of the 'Guernica', from the obvious rose of womanhood or the lily of chastity to the personal symbols of T.S. Eliot . . . (these) enter into the work of art as elements, creating and articulating its organic form. . . The meanings of incorporated symbols may lend richness, intensity, repetition or reflection or a transcendent unrealism. . . But they function in the normal manner of symbols.

Intentional symbolism enters the dance as soon as gestures have specific meanings which are vital elements in the dance structure. For example, a dance which has, as its main motif, 'rising-opening-turning-closing-sinking' will develop this idea as a theme with variations, perhaps, and all the gestures will be elements in the total pattern of the dance, but none of them will convey meaning beyond what is seen; the dancer's awareness will be concentrated entirely upon his own moving body in the dance, and the feelings of rhythm and flow and shaping which belong to it. But 'rising' can be a gesture of aspiration (towards a celestial power, perhaps); 'opening' – a gesture of welcome; 'turning' – one of out-going pleasure; and 'closing-and-sinking' – of withdrawal and submission; and with this meaning to be conveyed, the facial and bodily gestures are intentionally descriptive in character, the dancer's awareness extends beyond himself, and his movements 'stand for' his feelings in relation to the outside world.

The dancer also makes use of intentional symbolism when he dances as 'fire', as 'death', as 'the puppet' – or in any role other than his own. In each of these instances, he has taken as his stimulus an image which is not primarily a dance image, but which has enough about its actual or imagined movement qualities to make the transfer possible. This assumption of other roles is a particular feature of theatre dance; and it is interesting to observe that the theatre provides the context for a close association between the arts – but almost always with the visual effects enhancing the main content, (whether dance, drama, or music), and rarely with the various elements so interdependent that any one is meaningless when removed from the whole.

Finally, we come to the philosopher's consideration of the Art Symbol (as distinct from the symbol in art). Drawing upon a special theory of significance in music, as set out in her book 'Philosophy in a New Key', Langer (1960) says of any work of art that it is:

> . . . the image of feeling, which may be called the Art Symbol. It is a single organic composition, which means that its elements are not independent constituents, expressive in their own right, of various emotional ingredients. . . The elements in a work are always newly

98

created with the total image, and although it is possible to analyse what they contribute to the image, it is not possible to assign them any of its import apart from the whole. That is characteristic of organic form. The import of a work of art is its 'life', which, like actual life, is an indivisible phenomenon.

In the present context this, of course, immediately begs the question whether or not, by proposing to integrate or combine the arts, we are working towards a further organic whole? Or are we simply concerned with integrating or combining the art processes? If we have some hope of 'single organic compositions' arising through close association of the arts, is this a process for which we can educate others, or can we only provide a sympathetic context in which it has the best chance of occurring? If we are only concerned with combining or integrating the art *processes,* is our aim to increase the range of techniques available to each individual and familiarise them with several media? Or to enrich their imagery? Or to increase their expressive potential? If all of these, how shall we know when we are succeeding? The philosopher lays stress upon the art process, but in her terms the art process *contains* the final expressive form – the organic whole – the obvious measure of success. She (Langer, 1953) writes, in 'Feeling and Form':

> . . . the making of a symbol requires craftsmanship as truly as the making of a convenient bowl or an efficient paddle, and the techniques of expression are even more important social traditions than the skills of self-preservation. . . Technique is the means to the creation of expressive form, (which is) the symbol of sentience: the art process is the application of some human skill to this essential purpose. . . Art is the creation of forms symbolic of human feeling.

But then, there never was a problem of integration, re-integration, or combination for the philosopher; at this level, all arts are one in terms of symbolic expression (though feelings will be given form in different media by appropriate and specialised skills). But at the level of creativity, art begins with a particular act of perception already couched in terms of what techniques the artist has; and the acquisition of those techniques, right from the making of the first descriptive gesture or the first intentionally-repeated movement, occurs alongside the particular manner of looking (in the case of visual art) or interest in moving (in the case of dance). In other words, we see what we are ready to see, and feel what we are ready to feel. Education may lead us to see and feel with greater sensitivity; it may show us ways of blending the two experiences; but it cannot force in us new modes of perception requiring appropriate but undevised techniques, simply by proposing a new label—Integrated Arts.

Summary

In attempting to summarise the findings of this exploration, it may be helpful to consider certain lines of development in the individual which lead from the beginning of differentiation in the young baby to the mastery of technique and the creation of form in a particular medium. This 'linear' approach, whilst presenting an over-simplified view of a multi-dimensional development, does at least enable us to look more closely at areas in which divergence occurs, for it is at each point of divergence that we might 'look around', so to speak, at the forms of expression we already have, and be conscious of the art process which demands further refinement of the materials and techniques at our disposal.

The young baby moves, and, in moving, is expressive to the observer – though not at first intentionally so. One form of movement expression reveals a bodily state which is generalised and undirected – contentment, perhaps, or discomfort; the other, which develops through his needs and his growing awareness of cause and effect, becomes directed towards an end – a cry to be picked up and held, which later becomes a gesture of appeal; or the angry, sweeping dismissal of unwanted food or company. The first form of expression indicates self-awareness at the sensory level, with increasing sensitivity to touch and feel; to mobility and arrest; to stability and instability, and the achievement of a 'working' equilibrium; to the flow of the weight of the body in space; and to the rhythm of action and recovery. All this is fundamental to the centering of the self through movement awareness, and has no concern with others around – though an observer would be aware of the incidental bodily expression occurring, which Arnheim describes as 'physiognomic'. Such self-centering leads on to those kinds of self-rewarding activities (which may eventually become socialised when cooperation increases the interest) in which kinaesthetic awareness predominates – dancing and swimming, for example.

The second form of movement expression indicates an awareness of others, through demand and response, conflict and resolution, recognition and rejection – in other words, communication through intentional expression. It requires a participant, or an imagined participant, to whom emotional needs are directed – anger, desire, grief – and uses 'descriptive' movements (Arnheim) with which to communicate, mainly gestural (but often extended into the whole body), and leading later to mime and to characterisation, where the message or the role is of greater importance than the underlying rhythm or the incidental shape (though both these elements are present).

Implied in this second development is increasing sensitivity in seeing and hearing. At the same time, this sensitivity is the beginning of the management of the self in the external world – the apprehension of space, across which people and objects can be reached or propelled by means of movement. Eventually, it is possible for the child to think of *himself* as an object, so that the personal feeling of rising and stretching can also be understood as 'my body going high', and 'high' becomes a place to aim for in a jump, perhaps – a place which exists in relation to himself and to others, whether he is jumping or not.

So we have already a possible point of divergence – where the *intention* to be expressive develops alongside the *incidental* expression which arises in the very act of living. This divergence is not at first clearly marked, though it occurs very early on in the development of self-awareness. A second point of divergence along the original road occurs with the visual awareness of the shapes, forms, and spatial relationships arising from self-rewarding, kinaesthetically-motivated movements, which seem to the moving person to externalise his pleasurable feelings, or his mood, or the essence of an abstract idea ('angularity', 'violence') in visual form. Used with intention, these movements are also descriptive in character; but *shape* is of prime importance, and may be traced through the air or across a canvas, informed with whatever qualities give back to the mover the psychosomatic experience he seeks – lingering, pliant, delicate, with-holding, momentary, strong, on-going; in one situation the body itself (in gesture) is central to the created form; in the other, the body will lose its central role, and the picture will become the created form.

This is the road of the embryo artist, whether he be dancer or painter; but because the individual is moving forward in the two ways already mentioned, the artist's road is broadened by the developing perception of self, of others around him, and of the world of objects and events which make up his total experience. The shaping of movement ideas around a story concerning particular people who react to one another and to the events that overtake them leads to the creation of a dynamic art form – what we may call a dance-drama. The shaping of line, mass, colour and texture into forms that echo those in the environment leads to the creation of a visual art form for contemplation – a picture. And between these two roads is an area which is accessible from either, for the creation of a dynamic visual event, in which the role of the moving individual is entirely subordinate to the visual effect, as in some of the experimental works of Alwin Nikolais; and for action painting as shown by Jackson Pollock.

My self-imposed brief was to look at relationships between movement and painting, in order to understand better the nature of any relationship between dance and this one aspect of the visual arts. If it was not evident at the beginning of my task, it must by now be clear that I find the proposition for integration of the arts highly problematical – because, like many of my colleagues, I am already tutored in, if not conditioned to, certain traditional techniques in certain traditional media; I perceive in certain ways, and those ways are dependent upon the techniques already to hand – techniques which were taught by others who perceived in similar ways; or self-taught, to discover the utmost potential of a familiar material. My sensitivity and perception are tuned to the possibilities of rhythm, flow, line and colour particularly, shaped by a continuing dialogue between technique and material.

But new art forms – the product of integration – require new modes of perception arising from fresh techniques in dialogue with unfamiliar material; and this is probably not given to the practising artist, or to the teacher of art, but only to the untutored student and the young child.

References and Bibliography

REFERENCES

Arnheim, R. *Art and Visual Perception.* London: Faber & Faber, 1956.

Arnheim, R. *Towards a Psychology of Art.* London: Faber & Faber, 1966.

Burt, C. *Mental and Scholastic Tests.* London: Staples Press Ltd., 1921.

Goodnough, R. Pollock paints a picture. *Art News,* May, 1951.

Guillaume, P. *Imitation in Children.* Chicago: University Press, 1971.

Kellogg, R. *What Children Scribble and Why.* California: National Press, 1955.

Kellogg, W.N. & Kellogg, L.A. *The Ape and the Child*. New York: McGraw Hill, 1933.

Krotzsch. *Rhythmus und Form in der freien Kinderzeichnung*. Leipzig, 1917.

Laban, R. *The Mastery of Movement*. London: Macdonald and Evans, 1960.

Laban, R. *Modern Educational Dance*. London: Macdonald and Evans, 1963.

Laban, R. *Choreutics*. London: Macdonald and Evans, 1966.

Langer, S. *Philosophy in a New Key*. Cambridge, Mass.: Harvard University Press, 1960.

Langer S. *Problems of Art*. New York: Charles Scribner's Sons, 1957.

Langer, S. *Feeling and Form*. London: Routledge and Kegan Paul, 1953.

Lowenfeld, V. *Creative and Mental Growth*. London: Macmillan, 1964.

Morris, D. *The Biology of Art*. London: Methuen, 1962.

Piaget, J. *Play, Dreams, and Imitation in Childhood*. London: Routledge & Kegan Paul, 1951.

Piaget, J. & Inhelder, B. *Mental Imagery in the Child*. London: Routledge & Kegan Paul, 1970.

Pollock, J. In *Possibilities*. Ed. R. Motherwell and H. Rosenberg: New York: 1947/48 and quoted in O'Connor, Francis V. *Jackson Pollock*. New York: Museum of Modern Art, 1967.

Read, H. *Education Through Art*. London: Faber, 1958.

Robertson, B. *Jackson Pollock*. London: Thames & Hudson, 1960.

Sachs, C. *World History of the Dance*. London: George Allen & Unwin, 1938.

Tomassoni, I. *Pollock*. London: Thames & Hudson, 1968.

BIBLIOGRAPHY

Arnheim, R. *Visual Thinking*. London: Faber & Faber, 1970.

Best, D. *Expression in Movement and the Arts*. London: Lepus, 1974.

Collingwood, R.G. *The Principles of Art*. Oxford: Clarendon Press, 1938.

Dewey, J. *Art as Experience*. New York: Capricorn, 1934.

Eng, H. *The Psychology of Children's Drawings.* London: Routledge & Kegan Paul, 1931.

Ehrenzweig, A. *The Hidden Order of Art.* London: Weidenfeld & Nicolson, 1967.

Field, D. & Newick, J. *The Study of Education and Art.* London: Routledge and Kegan Paul, 1973.

Hospers, J. (Ed.) *Introductory Readings in Aesthetics.* New York: Free Press, 1969.

Klee, P. *On Modern Art.* London: Faber & Faber, 1958.

Klee, P. *The Thinking Eye.* London: Lund, Humphries, 1956.

Lange, R. *The Nature of Dance.* London: Macdonald and Evans, 1975.

Read, H. *The Meaning of Art.* London: Faber & Faber, 1931.

Reid, L.A. *Meaning in the Arts.* London: George Allen & Unwin, 1969.

Richardson, M. *Writing and Writing Patterns.* London: University of London, 1925.

Steveni, M. *Art and Education.* London: Batsford, 1968.

Vernon, M.D. *The Psychology of Perception.* Harmondsworth: Pelican, 1962.

Index

107